Praise for *Signs from the*

"Over the centuries, across the world, fr[...] to television mediums, human beings have sought to speak [...] deceased. However, is it truly possible to receive communications from beyond? Bill Philipps's book is an unpretentious exploration into after-life communication and offers illustrations and tools that tell readers that yes, indeed, it *is*. The book is a pleasure to read and will bring comfort to those who read it. I recommend that anyone interested in this topic read *Signs from the Other Side*."

— Raymond Moody, MD, PhD, author of *Life After Life*

"Witnessing Bill Philipps engage with people at countless live-audience readings and with listeners while in studio on our morning show never ceases to leave me in awe. I'm now even more astonished by his ability to seamlessly pour the same healing energy, insight, and empathy right onto the pages of his books. The stories Bill shares illuminate proof that signs from our departed loved ones are truly around us every day, everywhere!" — Evelyn Erives, cohost of *ODM and Evelyn in the Morning*, 99.1 KGGI (Riverside, California)

"How many times have you noticed an inexplicable coincidence or had an indescribable feeling that a deceased loved one was near? In *Signs from the Other Side*, Bill Philipps teaches you how to hone your in-tuition and recognize the subtle clues that the spirits of the dead are always sending us. Along the way, he narrates unforgettable stories about his own encounters with the spirit world, told with empathy and down-to-earth humor."

— Elisa Medhus, MD, author of *My Son and the Afterlife*

"In his book *Signs from the Other Side*, Bill Philipps writes about com-municating with Spirit in an accessible and refreshing manner that demystifies the topic. He informs readers that it is possible for all of us to witness communication from our beloveds in the simplest of ways — and invites all of us to see, hear, and feel the voices and presence of the ancestors all around us." — Lisa Smartt, author of *Words at the Threshold* and founder of the Final Words Project

"For many, a spiritual awakening first occurs when they hear a message from a loved one who has passed to the other side. It becomes an all-important doorway to contacting the universal energy we are surrounded by on a daily basis but have not been trained to see or connect with. In this book, Bill Philipps lovingly brings you, the reader, his gift of helping others make this connection. The stories and lessons in *Signs from the Other Side* remind us that there is more to life, and our relationships, than meets the eye. And when we open to that, magic starts to happen."   — Lee Harris, author of *Energy Speaks*

Praise for *Expect the Unexpected* by Bill Philipps

"An honestly refreshing glimpse into the world of mediumship and Spirit. Bill Philipps…empowers us all to tap into our own intuitive gifts and spiritual awareness."

— Rebecca Rosen, bestselling author of *Spirited*

"Part memoir, part spiritual exploration, part inspiring stories, *Expect the Unexpected* provides wisdom, knowledge, insight, and support for communicating with and tapping into spiritual realms we do not fully understand."   — *Psychic News*

"To read Bill Philipps's writing is to be held by his spirit. He is a force of goodwill on this earth, and he heals hearts….I am grateful for Bill Philipps. I am grateful for his book."

— Christine Woods, actress, *Hello Ladies* and *The Walking Dead*

"This beautifully written book is educational and enlightening — well worth reading for believers and skeptics alike."

— Gary E. Schwartz, PhD, professor, University of Arizona, and author of *The Afterlife Experiments* and *The Sacred Promise*

"Bill Philipps is not only a gifted psychic medium but one of the most sincere and genuine young men I have ever met. He brings healing and hope where there is loss and pain."

— Tanya Brown, author of *Finding Peace Amid the Chaos*

SIGNS
FROM THE
OTHER
SIDE

OPENING TO THE
SPIRIT WORLD

BILL PHILIPPS
with William Croyle

New World Library
Novato, California

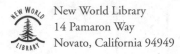

New World Library
14 Pamaron Way
Novato, California 94949

Text design by Tona Pearce Myers

Library of Congress Cataloging-in-Publication data is available upon request.

First printing, March 2019
ISBN 978-1-60868-552-3
Ebook ISBN 978-1-60868-553-0
Printed in Canada on 100% postconsumer-waste recycled paper

New World Library is proud to be a Gold Certified Environmentally Responsible Publisher. Publisher certification awarded by Green Press Initiative.

10   9   8   7   6   5   4   3   2

I dedicate this book to all of you who have lost someone you love. Look around you — and you will find that they have been right here with you all along.

Contents

Introduction:
If My Dad Can Do It...

I invited my dad to brunch one recent Sunday afternoon. We haven't always had the closest relationship, but fortunately it has strengthened with time. After a delicious meal and rich conversation, we were saying our goodbyes in the restaurant parking lot when a beautiful white butterfly fluttered our way. It danced in front of us, then circled us multiple times. It was obvious, at least to me, that it was trying to get our attention. I knew there was nothing random about its presence.

"Look at that," I said. "Mom is letting us know she is here with us." A split second after those words spilled from my mouth, I cringed. *Why did I just say that out loud?*

Faint hope, I guess. I braced myself for Dad's reply.

"Yes, she is," he said with sincerity in his voice as his eyes followed the butterfly's path.

I was stunned. And joyful beyond measure.

Anytime I had ever talked about receiving signs or other information from the spirit world, Dad laughed, joked, or scoffed.

For personal and religious reasons, he never could understand why I had passed on a surefire career as an opera singer in favor of one as a psychic medium. In his defense, what parent *wouldn't* find that incomprehensible? That's why those three words from him were such a breakthrough in his mind-set and in our relationship.

He knew that since Mom's death in 1999, when I was just fourteen years old, I had believed that white butterflies were a sign from her that she was with me. I don't know on this day in the parking lot how much Dad truly believed it, but it appeared he had at least unlocked his mind and heart to entertain the possibility that she was responsible.

And that is exactly how every opportunity to receive a sign from someone who has crossed over to the next life must begin.

Each day, spirits are trying to connect with us to help us make decisions, find meaning in our lives, or navigate through difficult times. They try to create that link in a multitude of ways, such as with animals, electricity, music, dates, numbers, dreams, and coins. They repeatedly dangle these things right in front of us, and though we see them, we usually consider them nothing more than ordinary objects or coincidences that have no significant meaning in our lives. That's because we don't know how to view them as something more, or we simply don't believe.

How often have you made a decision based on a gut feeling? Isn't the result of your decision usually the one you had hoped for or expected? And how often have you said to yourself, "Something is telling me I should [or shouldn't] do this"? That "something" is your innate psychic ability, commonly known as *intuition*. It is a God-given gift that is seized upon by the spirit world to help guide you in your earthly journey.

What we often fail to realize is that even though a dead person's body is gone, their spirit is not. Their soul lives, not just in heaven but on earth. Sure, we may comfort ourselves by saying that we know they are around us or that we feel their energy, but do we truly believe they are present in our lives to the extent that they can communicate directly with us from the beyond at any moment?

They *are*, and they *can*.

If your first reaction is "I need to see it to believe it," make a couple of adjustments to that phrase and you'll be right on track: "I need to *believe* it to *see* it."

One day, when I was trying to navigate through some difficulties in my life and desperately longed for my mom, I asked her to show me a sign that she was with me. Believing that she would, and paying close attention to my surroundings, I was expecting to see the usual white butterfly. But instead, I received something much more definitive.

The next day I found myself driving behind a car with a license plate that read "YVONNE" — my mom's name. Not only is that a relatively uncommon name, but there are millions of registered vehicles in the vast state of California and only *one* with that plate. How did I end up in that exact place on the road at that precise moment behind that car the day after I had asked for a sign? Coincidence? No way. I think my chances of winning the lottery might have been better. Signs from the spirit world are literally everywhere. Fortunately, I was in a frame of mind that enabled me to recognize one.

In a world fraught with uncertainty, people are often searching for guidance in an earthly form but struggling to find it, so they are turning more and more to the "other side" for help. I witness it daily from those who reach out to me for readings or advice, many of them desperate to connect with a loved one who has passed. But the good news is that you don't need me to make that connection. Yes, with a gifted medium as a conduit, communication between you and the spirit world will be much clearer. But neither I nor any other medium can be that conduit for everyone all the time. That is why if you believe in the intuition you were born with and are open to the possibilities, the spirits will take care of the rest directly with you.

I want to be clear that this is not a traditional mediumship book in the sense that it does not delve fully into the spiritualism aspects, technical terms, or history of mediumship. Every medium works differently and has their own belief system. This book reflects all the information I've learned over the years through sharing my gift with others. In short, this is my truth.

You will find the first few chapters to be a brief synopsis of my first book, *Expect the Unexpected: Bringing Peace, Healing, and Hope from the Other Side*. I highly recommend that before you dig into this book, you read *Expect the Unexpected* to get the vivid details of my background and the strongest confirmation of this gift I have been given. If you can't, the early chapters here should provide you with enough information to help you understand the ones that follow. In those following chapters will be specifics of how you can open yourself to receiving signs and how to recognize them, along with stories from people just like you who have experienced the beauty of their intuitive connection to those in heaven.

Think about those linked to your life who have died. Many of them have likely been sending you signs quite frequently and for a long time, signs that would reassure you they are okay, that might let you know they are watching over you and your family, or that could provide you with a solution to a problem. But you won't recognize them as signs without *believing* in them. Once you believe, your perspective toward everything that happens around you will change dramatically. Difficult times will become more peaceful, agonizing moments will be filled with more love, and mundane experiences will become glorious reminders that spirits are always with you to help you live a better life here on earth.

Trust me — if my dad can open his mind and heart to this possibility, you can, too.

Part I

WHO I AM
AND
WHAT I CAN DO

1 Surviving Childhood

No child says, "When I grow up, I want to be a psychic medium!" Even if they were to express that desire, it simply does not happen that way.

You won't find a psychic medium alongside a banker, lawyer, and veterinarian presenting to students at a school on career day. There is no high school aptitude test for your counselor to administer to help you decide if you would be best suited to the occupation of psychic medium. And it's certainly not a family business that you can inherit from your parents or grandparents.

You are selected to receive this gift, a gift the souls in heaven plant in your mind that evolves over time. Once the spirits know that you realize who they are and that you are willing and able to communicate their messages to their loved ones on earth, word spreads among them. Before you know it, your mind has become their sanctuary, and you have become their channel. They trust you, and they rely on you to convey their messages. Thus, a psychic medium is born.

The experience is very similar to what is depicted in the 1990 Oscar-winning movie *Ghost*. Whoopi Goldberg's character, Oda Mae, is a psychic, or at least she pretends to be one to try to make a living. Patrick Swayze plays Sam, who is shot and killed on the street in what appears to be a robbery attempt gone wrong, though it is actually a premeditated murder. After his death, Sam visits Oda Mae in her psychic shop; she can't see him, but she can hear him. He implores her to tell his girlfriend, Molly (played by Demi Moore), that he was murdered and that her life could also be in danger. It takes a lot of pestering by Sam for Oda Mae to accept that she really can hear a dead person, but after she does, and conveys his message to Molly, other spirits begin to appear to her on a regular basis to try to get her to relay messages to their own loved ones. They have found their channel in Oda Mae.

When it first happened to me, I denied it. I didn't believe it, and I didn't *want* to believe it. But once I knew it was real, I didn't want to let it go. I realized I'd been given a gift that could bring peace, happiness, and closure to people in ways that they otherwise couldn't experience. As burdensome as it was at times, it was a responsibility I felt I had to assume.

Before I go any further into how I do what I do, let me briefly share with you my bizarre upbringing and how this extraordinary life started for me. You will find many more details in my book *Expect the Unexpected*, but here is a summary to familiarize you with my background.

My parents both suffered with drug addiction before I was born, and the birth of their first child didn't change their habits. I was raised in Southern California in a toxic environment, a witness to abuse in many forms. The fact that I made it out of my childhood alive was a miracle.

Mom and Dad separated in 1991 when I was six years old. They got back together after a few months, but my mom secretly had a boyfriend. She devised a plan to kidnap me from my dad, and she followed through with it one day after he left for work. We fled to a friend's house, where we stayed until late in the evening as Dad drove up and down the neighborhood streets searching and screaming for us. Afraid he would find us, Mom dragged me to an abandoned school bus in a ditch, lit with gas lanterns. We hid there with her junkie friends, who were high on crack, jabbing themselves with needles, and performing sex acts on each other. I buried myself in the backseat of the bus with my ears covered and eyes squeezed tightly shut while Mom joined them.

The next day my mom, her boyfriend, and I boarded a Greyhound bus. We spent several days traveling cross-country to Brooklyn, New York, where her boyfriend had family. We lived there in various houses and apartments, and I often had to visit the closest church to get food since I didn't have any at "home." I didn't realize we were homeless, because I never slept on a street — but we were. I rarely had a bed. I often slept on floors in rooms with multiple people I didn't know. Once I was settled under my blanket for the night, Mom would give me a kiss, tell me she loved me, and then usually hit the streets for her drug fix. Sometimes she was home by morning; other times she wasn't.

I was shuttled back and forth between a couple of schools each year, depending on where we were living at the time. I managed to keep up my grades, though I'm not sure how, given the instability in my life. A lot of things I saw daily — drugs, guns, violence — scared the crap out of me, but given that it was all I had known since the day I was born, nothing surprised me.

I lived in New York for three years. My stay there ended when my mom's boyfriend's sister, who had been housing us and taking care of me anytime Mom was on a drug run, had had enough. She tracked down my dad, who was living and working in Las Vegas. She told him if he'd send a plane ticket, I was all his. He did.

I was happy to be with my dad, but the living arrangements were like those in New York. We spent about six months in an apartment in Vegas, where Dad struggled to make ends meet and continued to suffer with his addiction. We then moved back to Southern California and lived in different hotels. This transience continued for almost three years until I was twelve, when my grandma (my dad's mom) took me in to give me some stability for the first time in my life.

While living with my dad and grandma, I regularly kept in contact with my mom by phone. Despite what she had put me through, I loved her deeply, and I knew how much she loved me. Because of my dad's obvious distrust toward her, I wouldn't return to New York to visit her until August 1999, just a few weeks short of my fifteenth birthday and nearly six years after I had last seen her. I went back because her boyfriend called to tell me she had pancreatic cancer and was failing fast. She had mentioned to me a few days earlier that she had some medical issues, but she didn't let me know how dire they were because she didn't want me to worry. I caught a red-eye flight to New York on a Friday to see her. I arrived Saturday morning and went straight to the hospital.

That evening, alone with her in the room and with her hand in mine, I watched as she quietly passed away.

Two days after my mom's death, in the guest bedroom of an old home I was staying in on Long Island, I was awakened by a natural light in the far corner of the room. Actually, a *supernatural* light.

It was my mom.

She was young, beautiful, healthy, and happy — not the sickly, beaten-down woman I had just seen die in the hospital. When I realized that it was her and acknowledged her, she smiled. I couldn't believe what I was seeing, but I knew this was not a dream. I was awake, and she was there, like an apparition. She appeared to be more alive than *I* was at that hour.

"Billy, I want you to know that I'm okay," she said in a soft, soothing voice. "Also, know that I will take care of you."

And then she vanished.

I stayed awake for a while in case she returned, but she didn't. I continued to sleep in that room for the next couple of nights, hoping...but to no avail.

Within a few weeks after I returned home to Southern California, my dad suddenly began a yearlong journey toward quitting his drug habit. I know it was fueled by my mom's death, which bothered him a lot. He cried when I called from New York to tell him she had passed. They'd had some serious differences, but I always knew they loved each other, even when they didn't outwardly show it. Since the end of that year, my dad has been clean. I believe that when Mom said she would take care of me, this is what she meant. She helped my dad sober up, which was a very big deal for me considering I was only fifteen years old at that time and had just lost her. She couldn't take care of me in her earthly form because of her own drug addiction, but she made up for it when she entered her next life and helped Dad kick his addiction.

2 An Unlikely Path

Toward the end of the summer after my mom's death, I was walking through a strip mall in Southern California with some friends when we passed a psychic shop. The psychic came out and stopped me.

"Wow!" she said. "You have an amazing gift." She was moving her hands in the space around me, like she felt some sort of energy. I watched her as if she was out of her mind. "You should be doing what I'm doing. But the thing is…it's going to take you about three years to understand what I'm saying."

Was she serious? My friends and I had a good laugh and moved on.

But right on cue, three years later, just after my eighteenth birthday in October 2002, a weird thing began happening to me: I would go to bed each night with chills and a feeling that someone was in the room with me. I shared my experiences with my friend's mom, Rachel, who believed in the spirit world and was someone I had often turned to for advice. She was fascinated by my story and suggested that I visit a metaphysical shop nearby. I wasn't thrilled about the idea because I didn't put much stock in places like that. I initially resisted going, but since the strange feelings hadn't subsided, I decided to give it a shot.

On the night I went, the store happened to be holding a two-hour class on how to develop mediumship skills, or how to communicate with the deceased. The teachers immediately tagged me as someone with "an aura," something I shrugged off as nothing but a setup for a future sales pitch. As the youngest person there and one of the few not dressed like a gypsy, I was most concerned with where the exits were and how I could get the heck out of there.

But I reluctantly stuck with it, and two hours later, I could not deny that the aura existed. I went through two tests, one that measured my extrasensory perception, or ESP, and one that tested my ability to connect with someone or something through the energy of an object. Not only did I pass both with tremendous ease, but I boggled the minds of the instructors and every other person in the room. I even brought one woman to tears because I was able to connect her with her close friend who had died.

When I reported to Rachel what had happened, she was ecstatic. She tested me further by having me give a reading to her. The spirit that came through to me during that reading meant nothing to her, but she told me to be patient. About a week later, Rachel met with one of her business clients. Through casual conversation, she figured out that the spirit that had come through during my reading with her the previous week was connected to this client, so she eagerly set up a meeting between us.

That client's son had recently died. During my reading with

her, I found I was able to tell her specific things about him that nobody else knew, as well as give her direct messages from this spirit, who I felt was actually inside my mind telling me what to say. So, a reading I had given to Rachel had been meant for someone she knew, which taught me that those on the other side had the power to orchestrate meetings between two complete strangers — her client and me — in order to communicate their messages to their loved ones.

As intriguing and exciting as this was, I didn't drop everything and instantly become the channel that the spirit world obviously wanted me to become. As a recent high school graduate, I was about to start taking classes at the local community college, and I was going to continue voice lessons. I loved to sing, and I had been blessed with a rare operatic tenor voice. I was also working up to forty hours a week as a barista at a café. I decided to stick with the classes, lessons, and job while giving readings when I could. I figured, still being young, I had plenty of time to determine what I should — or was destined to — do with my life.

I worked on my psychic medium skills at the café by trying to determine the names of customers. I would pick them out of the line, ask the spirits for their names, and then ask the customers their names when they would come up to place their order. I listened for that inner voice from within, and nearly every time I was able to correctly name them or come awfully close. If I were completely wrong, I would usually discover that the name I had heard was that of someone else standing close by, such as next in line. Or I would learn that the name I had received wasn't that of the customer in line but rather of the actual spirit tied to that person.

I eventually took my gift to another café on my off days, not as an employee but as a customer. I would sit at a table and try to figure out names of other customers and of the staff. I tried to be discreet in these self-tests, but the times I did tell people what I was doing, my efforts were met with unbridled enthusiasm. I thought they would freak out and call me crazy, but instead they wanted more, and word of my gift quickly spread. Customers would try to time their visits to the café with mine and sit by me. Sometimes they would bring their friends in to "show me off." Servers would argue over who got to wait on me, with the hope that they could get a reading. I then began doing readings outside the café for many of the people there, meeting them in parks or in their homes, and they paid me for my time. This gift was taking on a life of its own, and it was taking over mine.

As a result, in January 2003, I left my job at the café. I enjoyed working there, but I was spread too thin and needed to give up something. With the readings providing me money for college and voice lessons, I made mediumship my job instead.

Every reading I gave increased my knowledge of the extent of my capabilities. Like anything else in life, the more I practiced this skill, the more I mastered it.

I learned that when I did a reading, I had to enter a trance-like state. Those on the other side were throwing information at me nonstop. Therefore, I needed to be laser-focused and share it immediately with my client as it came in. The message from the spirit was like the sound waves of music passing through a radio (me) to a listener (the client). I then had to help the client interpret it. When we were finished, it was necessary to completely disconnect myself from it so that I could psychologically prepare for the next reading. Each time, I expended an enormous amount of energy. If I hadn't consistently "discarded" each reading when it was finished, my brain would have crashed from the overload of information.

I also learned early on that those on the other side were often fighting for position in my mind so that I would hear their messages. If I was reading for a group, it was as if their deceased loved ones were pushing each other out of the way to get to the front of the line. It was my job to try to separate their energies, like untangling a bunch of cords. That is why in a group reading it would likely take me a while to figure out whom the spirit was trying to reach, and why I counted on the clients to help me determine that.

Something else I learned was that a message from a spirit did not always immediately make sense to a client, but it would with time. For example, if we had determined that a client's grandmother was coming through to us and she talked about some letters in a shoebox, the client might have had no idea what that meant: "Letters? I don't know anything about any letters." But that didn't mean the letters didn't exist and wouldn't materialize at some point in the future. The client and I both needed to trust what the spirit was saying, no matter how little sense it made at the moment. In time, if the client had an open mind and open heart, the message would become clear.

I continued with the readings, voice lessons, and school for the next couple of years, until January 2005 when I made a major decision: I was going to attend the prestigious San Francisco Conservatory of Music to train as an opera singer. A few months earlier, I had been among roughly a hundred candidates who auditioned for just one open spot at the school — and I got it. The faculty identified me as a "young dramatic tenor" with a very rare "young Wagnerian" voice. They viewed me as someone who had tremendous potential to succeed in the world of opera. As successful as I had been doing readings, this was an opportunity I could not pass up.

But guess where the spirit world goes when you decide to move to San Francisco? With you to San Francisco. The spirits couldn't have cared less about what my career plans were or that I was moving. I had been their channel, they trusted me, and they weren't going to let that go.

As it turned out, my time at the Conservatory sharpened my skills as a psychic medium in a couple of ways. One way was by singing onstage, which taught me how to handle pressure in front of audiences and to trust my talents. The other way was through the vibration of the music, which was very similar to the feeling I had when tuning in to spirits. Music can raise your energy and cut through any negativity you are experiencing. For me, music connected my energy with my soul and produced an exhilaration that helped me connect with the spirit world.

I cut back on readings when I got to the Conservatory, doing them mainly by phone for people back home or face-to-face when I returned to Southern California for breaks. The only person I initially did them for on campus was a teacher whom I had told about my gift. A spiritual person herself, she was so excited to hear about my ability that she wanted to help me develop it while I was in school, and I agreed to let her. She taught me how to "sing spiritually" by correlating the way I sang with the energy inside me, and she also had me give readings to specific opera teachers at the school and at other colleges who she knew would be open to my gift — and it worked.

In no time, I was doing readings for some of the top opera people in the world. They were blown away by my abilities, and I was soon doing multiple readings a week. It was exhausting, but I felt a real responsibility to keep doing it. As strange as it may sound, abandoning those souls that had crossed over would have been an ethical failing, in my opinion.

After graduating in the spring of 2008 at the age of twenty-three, with an opera degree in hand, I decided to set it aside to pursue a full-time career as a medium. I still had a passion for singing but not at the same level as I did for creating a connection between the dead and the living. My singing might affect someone's life for the moment, but my readings were changing lives forever.

I built a website by the fall and sent an email about my decision to all my family members and closest friends. Well, all except my grandma and dad. I needed to tell them in person, because I expected they were not going to be happy about my decision. Unfortunately, I was correct. My dad called me the devil and said I was a fool for not pursuing opera. Considering the sordid life he had led, I had hoped for a little more understanding from him, but there was none. My grandma at least listened to me, but she wasn't pleased either. She was a devout Christian who believed that mediumship was not something to be messed with.

The irony, from my perspective, was that she had raised me as a Christian, to believe in and emulate Jesus, a healer and an

21

instrument of love and peace. Providing emotional and spiritual healing for people by bringing peace and love into their lives through a connection with their deceased loved ones was my goal. How could I follow Christ any better?

What Grandma had taught me as a child about Christianity was the basis for what I was doing. I understood that the Bible said to stay away from mediums, but I couldn't deny this unique gift — and yes, I believed it *was* a gift, because how could something that was bringing such joy to people be anything else? I wasn't dabbling in Ouija boards or communicating with evil spirits. I knew I was doing the right thing, and I was doing it with nothing but pure and good intentions. I felt a responsibility to use this gift to bring happiness to as many people as possible, no matter who disagreed with me, even the woman I loved the most.

3 Making the Connection

Now that you know the gist of my background, I want to provide you with one last chapter of information condensed from *Expect the Unexpected* that will help you understand how I do what I do, which in turn will help you tap into your intuition more frequently and effectively.

First, you should know the difference between a *psychic* and a *medium*:

- All mediums are psychics because, like everyone else, they are born with an intuitive sense.
- A medium has to be a psychic because they use their psychic abilities to connect with and channel the spirits.
- Not all psychics are mediums because they do not necessarily communicate with the dead.

I have both abilities. As a psychic, I am "tuning in" to the energy of the spiritual side; it's like trying to find a radio station through static. Once that connection has been established, as a medium, I am "channeling" that spiritual energy and letting the information I receive flow through my psychic senses, which I can then share with others.

The reason we all have psychic abilities on some level is because we are all *spiritual* beings before we are *human* beings. The body is a shell that will eventually shut down once the heart stops pumping. The spirit, however, is the soul in each of us that lives forever. It is when we are alive in that shell on earth and we align our physical side with our spiritual side — that process of "tuning in" — that we can tap into our intuition.

I want to be clear that after reading this book you will not have the abilities of a medium, and even though you should be able to better tap into your intuition, your psychic abilities will not be at the level of mine unless you have been given this same gift. But they should be at a level higher than you have ever experienced.

Also, don't fall into the trap of believing the common misconception that anyone who is a psychic should know *everything*. That is absolutely not true. Psychics are not God, God does not want us to know everything (life wouldn't be much fun if we did!), and God gave every one of us free will to make decisions — good and bad — that can potentially change the course of our day and someone else's. The signs we receive from the spirit world are simply meant to be used as guides in our decision making or to bring us comfort during difficult situations.

While my intuition about something can be so strong that I could almost guarantee it is going to happen, it will never be a 100 percent guarantee, because we are beings who were created to think for ourselves and make our own decisions — again, free will. If I tell you something is going to happen to you, often you can determine whether it really comes to pass or not by the decision you make. So, then, why don't my psychic abilities allow me to know the decision you were going to make? Because there are more than seven billion people in the world, and I do not have access to their brains. Our psychic abilities can guide us well, but they cannot control our futures.

When I give someone a reading, the first thing we need to do together is validate who is coming through. This isn't always easy — the signs are not always clear — but it is often the most exciting part of the process because it is when the client realizes for certain that their loved one is really with us.

I may say, "I feel a strong mother connection who wants me to connect to the month of November. Do you understand?"

The client may respond, "Yes, my mom passed away two years ago in November, and my son's birthday also happens to be around this date."

In a private reading, the energy builds continuously. As a spirit from the other side makes the connection through me, they will start to validate more when they know their loved one sitting in front of me is understanding the flow of information. I fully surrender what *I* feel someone should receive, and I trust that what comes through is meant for this person in that moment and moving forward.

Not all those on the other side communicate in the same manner. Some come through so crystal clear to me that, without hesitation, I can identify their names and many other pieces of

Signs from the Other Side

information about them at lightning speed. Others aren't so easy to discern or understand.

When a spirit taps into my mind, it will usually bring up memories or associations in my life that will help the client and me validate who they are. If I am flashed a vision of my own dad when I am channeling a client's father from the other side, that spirit will most likely have the same name as my dad, Bill. But it could mean instead that the dad is acknowledging his son named Bill, or someone else on the other side with the name Bill who would be connected to the client. This is why communication with spirits can be challenging. But when I let my feelings and intuition flow as an undercurrent with the spirits, good things usually happen.

When information or signs flow through the channel from the other side to me, I receive them through one or more of the six spiritual senses:

- **Clairvoyance:** the ability to see with our "inner eye," beyond the human eye
- **Clairaudience:** the ability to hear beyond the human ear
- **Clairsentience:** the ability to feel or touch a spirit
- **Clairgustance:** the ability to taste beyond our human sense
- **Clairalience:** the ability to smell beyond our human olfaction
- **Claircognizance:** the ability to know without a reason (what people describe as a "gut feeling")

I usually won't see a deceased person standing in front of me or hear their actual voice. However, I certainly saw my mom after she died, and I've definitely seen spirit apparitions on other occasions, but these have usually been earthbound spirits. The communication normally happens through one of the clairs. The following is a brief description of each. Claircognizance is likely the one you will use most often, but it will be good for you to know all of them so that you can recognize them if they arise.

Clairvoyance is when the spirits insert messages into my mind using images of their choice. My soul then shows me those images, which I relay to the person during the reading. Some mediums call clairvoyance a "download" of information. When you download something onto your computer, there is normally a graphic that shows the pieces of the file being transferred. The percentage of completion quickly goes up until it hits 100. That's how rapidly the spirit world can throw information at me. It is rare for a spirit to just give me a straight message.

I've learned over time that the spirit world is using my own life experiences, memories, and lessons as a language to communicate with the living. Clairvoyance is a lot like playing charades; I have to trust every random image that comes through. My interpretation may not always be what that particular spirit is trying to convey, but I know that if I just say what they're showing me, it will eventually connect the puzzle pieces in divine time.

An example of this is a reading I gave to someone in which a mother was coming through. After a few minutes of channeling the way in which she died, I got an image of the month of June on a calendar, so I said, "She keeps showing me the month of June. Does that mean anything to you?"

I figured maybe her mother was born or died in June. But, to my surprise, the client excitedly replied, "Her name was June!"

I do wish spirits would be more straightforward with me —

that they would just tell me directly and clearly who they are and what they want to say. And sometimes they do, as you will read when I discuss claircognizance. But oftentimes they do not. I guess when I join them one day on the other side, I will find out why that is.

Clairaudience occurs a little more frequently in my readings than the remaining four clairs, especially through music. I once had a family come in for a reading, and the song "Angel" by Sarah McLachlan was playing in my head. I knew the song, and I knew it wasn't my own consciousness playing it, because it had been a long time since I had heard it. It turned out the daughter in that family had recently died and was named Angel.

With clairaudience, I also hear names or sounds that I have to phonetically piece together. For example, I was giving a reading once and I heard *Jane* in my mind. It wasn't the clearest, but when I said it, the client told me her name was Jean. As you can see, it's not always an exact science, but it's pretty darn close.

Clairsentience generally refers to spirits impressing their feelings into my feelings, usually in a way that shows me how they died. In other words, I may get a heavy sensation in my lungs to validate that the cause of death was lung cancer, or pressure on my chest signifying it was a heart attack.

Clairgustance and *clairalience* often occur simultaneously in my readings, and both usually involve food. If you and your deceased husband were regulars at a local Italian restaurant, I may taste Italian food, or if he was a gardener, I may smell certain herbs or fresh vegetables. Or I might smell cigarette smoke if the deceased person was a smoker in life. Smells of flowers or perfume sometimes come up, too. These two clairs come through to me less than the other four, but they are surefire validations when they do.

Claircognizance is the most fascinating of the clairs to me because it is all about simply knowing something. I don't see or hear or feel or taste or smell. I just *know*. For example, if you are going through a divorce, the soul communicating through claircognizance will just put that knowledge into my mind without flashing any pictures. If you were in a car accident, they will simply make me aware of that fact without my feeling the physical pain of impact. It is presented to me in an instant without any guessing games or fanfare. It's just a knowing.

Claircognizance is probably what you will experience the most when you are trying to receive signs from the other side, though it won't necessarily be in the same way or at the level I experience it. If your friend was just diagnosed with cancer, that likely will not instantly be divulged to you. But what your intuition *will* tell you is whether something you are experiencing is a sign from the other side.

For example, if you are driving down the road thinking about your deceased mother and her favorite song is the next one to come on the radio, you will know she had something to do with it. If you are out to lunch on your deceased grandpa's birthday and your check comes to $19.42, and he was born in 1942, you will know he is there with you. If you are taking a walk, sad about your friend who recently passed, and a beagle you have never seen before sprints past you, and your friend's favorite dog was a beagle, you will be comforted knowing that she is walking with you.

As you have probably figured out by now, there is one requirement when it comes to being able to receive signs from the other side: you have to believe. No, you don't have to have a deeply rooted faith in a certain religion or be a biblical scholar. You don't have to attend church or conceive of God the same way your neighbor might. But you *do* have to believe that your loved ones are in a spiritual form on the other side — which to me is heaven — and that even though their bodies are gone from this earth, their souls and energy are not.

Some don't believe in a life beyond this one because of the way they were raised or the influences around them. The signs from their loved ones will still be there — but, unfortunately, with closed minds and hearts, they will never see them for what they are and view them only as mere coincidences.

Open your mind, open your heart, and believe...and experience the beauty that unfolds around you.

Part II

SIGN, SIGN, EVERYWHERE A SIGN

4 Believe It Can Happen

We all have different beliefs in terms of the life beyond this one, beliefs cultivated over the years by *who* raised us and *how* we were raised, what we were taught, which part of the world we live in, which schools we attended, what we watch, what we read, and whom we listen to. Who or what you say is "God" or the "universe" may be completely different from my view. Even two people who sit next to each other in church week after week aren't necessarily going to have identical beliefs. But those differences are not important when it comes to recognizing signs from the other side. Anyone can do it. The only belief we have to share is that it's *possible* to receive those signs.

Many people, out of curiosity, ask me about my beliefs. You may find my faith a bit complicated, but I can tell you that it is based on the Christian upbringing my grandma provided. No matter your denomination, you will likely find some commonalities between what I believe and what you believe.

In order to understand my belief system, first you need to

understand my grandma. Although I know she loves me — the boy she raised and the man I've become — she does not love the part of me that you know, the medium. I honestly think it scares her. It flies in the face of her own belief system. As a devout Christian, she always keeps a Bible nearby. She prays daily and isn't afraid to preach the word of God publicly. And it is her courage to speak her beliefs that I so deeply admire and respect about her and cherish so dearly. When I was young, she would put on Bible-based cartoons for me to watch, and I enjoyed them. She is very "old-school" when it comes to her religion. She has lived her life with integrity and honesty, and she no doubt has earned her ticket to heaven.

She has never felt comfortable with my work as a medium because the Bible says to steer clear of communicating with the dead. She believes that the devil is somehow behind what I believe is my God-given gift. She doesn't believe *I* am the devil, as my dad once suggested long ago. She believes that the devil is tricking me and using me by posing as good spirits to try to infiltrate the lives of others. For example, if I tell you that your mom is coming through to me, my grandma would say it's really the devil *pretending* to be your mom in order to gain clearer access to you. This is completely false, and it comes from a place of fear. People often ask me if I am ever contacted by dark forces. The answer is no, because I protect myself with the white light of God before channeling.

While I completely understand my grandma's perspective, I obviously don't agree with it in light of my personal everyday experiences, all of them positive. I am convinced that God — a very loving God — gave me this ability and that I am doing what the Bible says with respect to using my God-given gift to serve others. In fact, this gift has not only helped those I share it with grow in their faith; it has helped *me* grow stronger in mine. My relationship with God has become more personal, I have learned how to pray, and I have realized that I am under an obligation to share this beautiful gift with the world.

So, what do I believe?

I believe in a spirit world called heaven that we enter when we leave our physical bodies behind on earth. Heaven is a spectacular place, but we enter it at different levels based on the lives we live as humans — what lessons we learned and those we failed to learn. The better people we are on earth, the better our position in heaven. However, I also believe we can move up levels once we are in heaven by acknowledging the errors we made when we were in human form, which are much more easily recognizable once our souls are separated from our bodies. We go through a life review to see how we could have done things differently and where we could have been more godlike, compassionate, and loving. Just as we learn, grow, and evolve while in the flesh, we continue to do so in spirit form.

I believe in reincarnation — that we all lived many lives before this one. I see earth as a classroom that was set up for us when we were in spirit form, where we chose which lessons our souls would benefit from, before incarnating into human form. We created a road map of sorts that detailed the experiences we could have in this life. That road map has many avenues, and because of free will, our decisions influence which is taken. Ultimately, which path we take can affect whether we fulfill our purpose and learn the lessons we were supposed to learn in this life. I believe that any "déjà vu" we experience is a quick snapshot of that road map, a confirmation that we are in sync with what we had planned our earthly experience to be.

I believe each of us is part of a preplanned soul group. For example, before you were born into this life, you made an agreement with your soul group, souls you traveled with in previous lifetimes. Those souls include blood family — parents, siblings, children, and so forth — along with non–family members. Together, you are all soul mates.

We generally refer to our romantic partner as a "soul mate," and they could be, but a soul mate could also be your good friend Bob from high school with whom you have a strong connection. It could be a teacher who had a profound effect on your life. It could be a neighbor who becomes your best friend over time. Soul mates are usually people who bring you feelings of connection and peace and love. A soul mate, however, could also be an alcoholic ex-husband who abused you but whose behavior taught you lessons about self-worth. We came into this life to learn those lessons and to grow from them.

Sometimes learning the lessons we need to learn in life requires a little help. I believe that spirit guides play a significant role in influencing our path. Spirit guides can be those who have transitioned to the afterlife but may not necessarily be anyone whom we've known in this life or who is part of our own soul group — although they can be. It is their duty to guide us and support us in specific circumstances. We are all given a spirit guide at birth and can gain more guides as we age. Spirit guides will help us through bumps in the road, trials, and tribulations, especially when our loved ones who died cannot help us.

For example, if you are having serious money problems and your late father, who could never manage his finances when he was on earth, is the only person close to you who has passed, your spirit guide would be the one to help you. If your father couldn't manage money here, he is not going to be the person on the other side you will want to call on.

I also believe in angels, beings that have never been in the physical body. They have always been in heaven and are the lightest and highest vibration of energy. We all have a connection with them, and they offer us a guiding hand in our lives and can make miracles happen. For example, if you have ever escaped death, chances are that an angel had something to do with that. Each angel is specific to a different theme. Michael the archangel is one you may have heard of. In the Bible, he is called on multiple times to protect people from evil. So, when we need protection, Michael is one angel who may be helping us.

I do believe in Jesus, a prophet sent here to offer us universal lessons of love and coming together. Christ is what many have called an "ascended master" — someone who was a highly evolved being who came here to help teach us the lessons we are here to learn, much in the same vein as Buddha or Gandhi.

I do not believe that God is an individual man or being above all in heaven (that is, God the Father) but more of a universal power that is limitless. We all make up the web of this greater power in both the physical and nonphysical forms, but in the physical form, our egos make us feel separate from one another. However, we truly are connected and always have been since the beginning of time. So you and I; your grandma, grandpa, mom, dad, and friend; your friend's aunt; and everyone else make up God. We are all one. But it is when we cross over to the other side and enter our nonphysical forms that we recognize that unity. We all are born from the same spiritual fabric — love — and we all return to that same spiritual fabric in heaven.

So, in a word, God is *love*.

I understand that if you are Catholic, Baptist, Muslim, Jewish, or any other religion, you are not going to agree with everything I've just stated. Hopefully, though, you can see some beliefs we all share, the primary one being that the foundation for our existence is love.

As I've mentioned, no matter what your beliefs, all you need to be able to recognize signs from heaven are an open mind and heart.

Opening your mind to receiving signs simply means believing it can happen. If you have faith in God or in the next life, you are already ahead of the game. If you don't have a deep-rooted faith in God or in anything else, don't fret; you can still do this. How? By detaching yourself from your ego and rational mind for a period of time.

When it comes to receiving signs, our egos and rational minds do us a disservice by trying to find logic in the most incredible messages from the other side rather than accepting those validations for what they are. Set aside any cynicism, any doubts, any preconceived notions, and be open to the possibility that there is something larger than yourself, a kind of energy that is simply above and beyond the human or material.

That energy can be a gut feeling. We all have intuition. You no doubt have gone with your gut when making an important decision, and you have trusted it. That feeling is guidance from God and the spirit world. It's that part of your soul that is connected to divine knowledge and wisdom, which can be attained by disengaging yourself from your ego and fear-based thinking. Even if you don't think of spirits as being the source, you can still understand this feeling to be an energy inside you that is instinctual and that you know has guided you in the past and you have been able to trust.

You can believe in the energy of the universe, an intangible force around us that comes from the stars, the planets, the galaxy. You may not believe that God is behind any of it, and that's okay — as long as you believe there *is* an energy beyond the scope of human life that is greater than you and me.

Another type of energy you can tune in to that can open your mind, one that many people don't think of as an energy, is *confidence*. Whether you are a superstar basketball player, a dentist, a mechanic, or a famous singer, when you tap into the energy that enables you to perform at your highest level, your gifts shine. If I am not in a confident mind-set, I won't be a clear channel to give effective readings. Like an athlete who needs to stretch, I have to warm up my mind, which I do through meditation and other methods (which I will share in a moment). The more I warm up, the more my confidence level increases, which puts my mind into a positive and open space.

So, is there any hope for an atheist to receive signs from the other side? Well, that would be difficult to do, considering an atheist doesn't believe there *is* an "other side." But here is an interesting story to ponder.

A friend of mine told me about one of his friends who is a hard-core atheist. This friend had always been adamant that there is no God or spiritual world or life of any kind beyond this one, and he wouldn't hesitate to debate anyone on the subject — which is what makes this story so fascinating.

Two days after a natural disaster had occurred in his community, he was volunteering his time at a local organization he belonged to. The organization was a very well-respected non-profit known for its charity work. In the case of this disaster, he and other volunteers there were accepting donations of clothes and then sorting them and distributing them to families in need. When his work was finished at the end of the day, he was reflecting on what he had experienced, and he was deeply moved by all that had been accomplished and by the outpouring of love and support from donors and volunteers. He was so moved, in fact, that he said that throughout the day he had felt the presence of the long-deceased people who had founded the organization years earlier, as if they had been watching over him and the other volunteers. It was the first time my friend had ever heard him allude to the possibility that there was something beyond this life.

Was he no longer an atheist after that feeling? No. His beliefs, or *non*beliefs, hadn't changed at all. But he certainly felt *something* or he wouldn't have made that comment.

To me, there is no question that those founders were there with him and the others. His feeling was real. Unfortunately, he probably released that feeling soon after it arose, listening instead to his rational mind. But it's proof to me that even those who may think there is no such thing as a spirit world are part of that spiritual web I talked about, whether they know it or not. Had he continued to let that door open wider when he felt what he'd felt, rather than allowing his ego to slam it shut, it potentially could have changed his worldview.

Signs are always right in front of us. Your loved ones who have passed have probably already sent some your way today. But, without an open and aware mind, they will be useless. It is much like having a conversation with someone. If I explain something to you and you sincerely listen to me, you will understand what I am saying. However, if I tell you something and you don't listen, my words will still be there, but they will have no effect on you, because you didn't pay attention.

Some things you can do to help you open your mind to be more aware of the other side and your psychic senses are pray, repeat affirmations, and meditate.

Prayer is the personal and intimate relationship we have with God, or whatever our higher power may be, to communicate our current and future hopes and desires. Simply put, it is talking to God. Prayer, as it relates to this book, is a way to communicate with our deceased loved ones, asking them to show us signs that they are with us. Everyone who believes in something greater than themselves prays in some way. Even those who say they do not believe in anything will often engage in a form of prayer without really knowing it.

I often see nonbelievers on social media say "Please send good vibes" or "Positive thoughts are appreciated" for intentions they post about. They don't want to use the term *prayer*, because they automatically connect prayer with God or some other form of energy beyond this life. But even in cases where they are putting forth an intention without calling on a specific higher power, an inner dialogue is taking place that I would classify as a form of prayer.

Prayer connects us to our highest good and to our intuitive selves. It is like casting a fishing net into the ocean, trying to catch something nourishing in its depths. Prayer is a way for us to set our intention.

How can you use the guidance of spirits for your benefit? It can be as simple as saying to your deceased grandmother, "Grandma, I need your help…" That request will lift your energy and vibration from your earthly mind-set to a higher, spiritual level.

In the physical form, we are going to experience difficult times and negative thoughts. We are programmed as human beings to always be in survival mode (or worry mode), thinking ahead about money, safety, work, shelter, and where our next meal will come from. That fear is part of our human fabric. But we always can tune in to the love of the other side, the love of God, which truly does transform our thinking into the positive. Those fearful thoughts are reminders to use prayer to plug back into the space of universal love, where anything is possible.

If your mom is very ill and the prognosis is not good, the immediate thought of losing her from your life would obviously be worrisome and stressful. But if you pause that negative thought for a moment to pray — to surrender that which you cannot control to the other side and to watch for signs of comfort — you will be able to see through the darkness that has shrouded you. Maybe, as you are holding your mom's hand while she lies in her hospital bed, you hear a song playing in a nearby room that she and your deceased father used to call "their" song. Or maybe the nurse who comes into the room to take care of her has the same unusual name as your mother's deceased sister. Perhaps one of the numbers on the monitors she is hooked up to reflects the date of your parents' wedding anniversary. These could all be signs that you would have never noticed without praying to your father or aunt.

Prayer is how we invite spirits on this journey with us and ask them to provide the stepping-stones we need to get to a space of truth. When we live in our truth, we can change our course for the better, but we need to be clear on what that road looks like first. Otherwise, we will go in circles throughout life without any real direction.

An *affirmation* is a declaration that, with repetition, can transform our thought process, better our emotional state, and raise our vibration. All change begins in the subconscious mind. An example could be the word *love*. When you think of the word *love*, it should stir positive emotions. When you say it repeatedly, it should make you feel blissful, connected, supported, and beautiful, overwhelming any negative thoughts or feelings you may have.

When you wake up in the morning, a great way to begin your day is with a positive intention, picturing yourself going through your activities surrounded by the light of God that will guide you to miracles and blessings and protect you from harm and evil. You can then "supercharge" your intention by using affirmations to help maintain your positive mind-set. If you are seeking confidence for something you have to do, tell yourself "I am confident now." If you are trying to lose weight, tell yourself "I am grateful for the weight I have lost, and I am going to continue on this journey today."

Being aware of the words we use makes a difference. It is a way to program our minds while, at the same time, sending a positive signal to our higher power that this intention is what we want, similar to prayer.

In terms of recognizing signs from the spirit world, an affirmation you might repeat if you need some strength from your deceased mother could be "Mom, I know you are with me today.

I am open to receiving signs from you, and I trust they will bring me the comfort and strength I need now." By setting an intention to hear from her in spirit, you automatically cast the net into unlimited possibilities of how she may present a sign that she is near and well.

There is never a guarantee of how we will receive that sign, but once the request is made, those on the other side work in miraculous ways to show us that they are around. The more aware we become, the easier it is to recognize these signs.

I mentioned in the introduction that I had asked my mom to show me a sign that she was with me while I was going through a difficult time. But I didn't just stop there. I continued to think of her in a very positive light and talk to her all day and into the night, keeping my eyes open for any kind of sign. The next day was when I saw the license plate with her name. I certainly wasn't looking for a message in a license plate, but I was looking for *something* from her. The repeated affirmations helped me recognize it.

It's not a bad idea to say every now and then, "I am aware of the signals and signs from the spirit world, and I trust myself more in acknowledging them now," or something along those lines. While I believe that spirits can sense when you are in tune with them, it can't hurt to verbally let them know, just to be sure.

Meditation is very similar to prayer, though it is more about *listening* than talking to God. It is about bringing inner peace, stillness, and focus to your mind rather than making a personal request to a higher power. It can involve techniques such as deep breathing, chanting, or simply sitting in silence to connect with the center of your soul.

The practice of meditating to de-stress was once regarded

by mainstream society as nothing short of absurd, and it still is today by some who have never tried it or explored its potential benefits. Those who don't understand it may also view it as a time waster that can slow down productivity at work, school, or home, or as a sign of weakness: if they can "make it" through the day without meditating, then everybody should be able to. But science has proved again and again that meditation can significantly improve our short- and long-term productivity and our overall effectiveness by strengthening our mental and physical capacities.

Studies on meditation have revealed that it can increase our focus, improve our ability to multitask, give us better control over our emotions, decrease depression and stress, boost our immune systems, and lessen our physical pain — all of which, of course, can open our minds to recognizing signs from the other side.

There is no one way to meditate. Meditation, like prayer, isn't limited to a particular place, time of day, or duration. You don't have to be sitting in a relaxed position in the center of a quiet room with the warm rays of the morning sun and a light breeze streaming through your open window (though that sounds lovely). People meditate by writing, exercising, or chanting. They meditate at home, at their desk at work, in a dressing room before a concert, or in a locker room before a game. They meditate as soon as they wake up in the morning, before bed in the evening, or in the afternoon while their children are napping. They meditate for intervals as short as a minute or as long as their day is, depending on the time they have or what their culture or religion dictates.

The key to successful meditation is removing all distractions

— those that are physically around you *and* those cluttering your mind. The more ego you can eradicate, the more space within your mind for the work of spirits around you to be recognized. Even with those distractions removed, meditating can be frustrating at first because your mind will wander. That's okay. This is new to you. Just allow the process to unfold. Let your thoughts gently flow through your consciousness and out of your mind. Don't force it. When you force it, you negate the purpose, which is to be in the moment.

There is a meditation in *Expect the Unexpected* that I have used quite frequently. You can also find many simply by searching online. Eventually, if you meditate enough, you will be able to develop your own meditation, one tailored to your specific tastes and available time.

Here is another example of a meditation you can try:

Close your eyes and focus on your breath.

As you inhale, notice the air traveling down your torso and filling your entire being. Hold it for a second.

As you exhale, feel all tension leave your body, sending it the signal for pure relaxation.

Again, inhale and hold it for a second. As you release your breath, surrender anything that sits heavy on your heart — sadness, anger, guilt, fear. It will not serve you. Let it all go.

Now, visualize a crystal-clear white light entering from the ceiling above you. (If you can't visualize this clearly, just set the intention that it surround you. In time, this will become like second nature.)

See this white light flow down like a waterfall and enter the top of your head, filling it with light and clearing away any negativity that stands in your way, blocking you from aligning with the unconditional love and energy from the other side.

With each breath, feel this white light continue to travel down through your head, your neck, your shoulders.

See and feel this light travel into your chest area, specifically into your heart.

Feel the white light connect with your heart chakra, and ask for your heart to be opened to the unconditional love of the spirit world.

Once you feel this connection, continue allowing this light to travel down your torso and legs, through your feet, and into the earth.

Feel that connection to the earth, the universe, spirits, and the divine energy that is God.

Once you feel this flow, ask that it surround you and protect you throughout your day so that you may be an extension of God's love all day long, living with compassion for others and accepting others.

Sit here for a few moments, until you feel completely present and centered. Allow this light to recharge your soul, which will positively affect your mind and body.

After a few more moments, when you feel ready, mentally bring yourself back to the room and open your eyes. Wiggle your toes to be sure you are fully back in your body and it is physically safe to get up.

Now, go about your day with this newfound energy, recharging at other points with the same meditation or a similar one if you feel you need it.

The most beautiful aspect of spirits is that they don't discriminate. Every single one of us has multiple connections with the other side — those who will listen to us, who will guide us, who will help us with whatever we need. It's very similar to our lives here on earth. There are people who will listen to, guide, and help us, but we are not going to recognize them for who they are if we close ourselves off from them, if we don't allow them into our lives to be of service to us. If we don't open our minds to those on the other side, they will still be there showing us signs, but it will all be in vain because we aren't letting them in. If we do open our minds, it will feel like we have opened up a whole new world outside the physical one we live in each day — because we *have.*

5 Recognizing Signs

How beautiful it would be to be able to say to your deceased mother, "Mom, I really need to know you're with me right now; will you please appear before me so that I can see you?" — and then watch as she appears.

Unfortunately, that's not how spirits operate. Any signs you receive from the other side likely will not be presented in the most obvious ways. But they won't necessarily be as subtle as you may think. It depends primarily on your mind-set and whether you are looking for them. If you surrender your expectations of how the signs may be presented and are vigilant about paying attention to your surroundings, you *will* recognize them. When you are on the lookout, your psychic senses will kick in, because that is where your energy is being directed.

Spirits will also try to send signs that you will relate to and avoid sending ones that you won't. The reason, of course, is because they *want* you to recognize them. For example, if you are a construction worker or a sports fanatic, they may send signs that relate to either of those things. If you are not into sports and aren't familiar with, say, basketball star LeBron James, your deceased mom will likely not send you something that has to do with LeBron. I am not into sports much at all, so when I give readings, it is rare for me to receive a detailed sports symbol as validation. Those on the other side know I'd get frustrated if I did. That doesn't mean they won't show me a particular sports object or something generically sports related; it's all relative to you and your knowledge base. In a reading I recently gave, the client's friend who came through had been a professional basketball player, and he kept showing me a basketball to validate that. But if he had shown me the logo of his former team, I'd have been lost.

There really are no limits with respect to how signs will be presented to you, but I am just going to briefly touch on some of the most common ways here. You will read many compelling examples of them in the "True Testimonies of the Spirit World" section that follows.

Dreams: When we sleep, our souls are working on the other side — taking a "time-out," of sorts, from this world — to help us focus on soul lessons that will need our attention when we awaken. Our dreams are rarely literal — a dream of a plane crash doesn't mean we will be in a plane crash or witness one. But we may need to decipher the meaning behind it, just like any other sign from the spirit world. There are many wonderful guides and books out there to help us translate the "language" of dreams so that we can unlock their messages. If you have an actual visitation from a loved one in a dream, you will know it. It will leave you feeling uplifted, loved, and supported. Sometimes they have no words at all and just smile at you, while other times they may tell you they are okay and not to worry. I've heard reports of full dialogues from clients, but typically these visitations are short and sweet.

Coins: It is very common for our loved ones on the other side to use coins to let us know that they are around us. I find that pennies seem to be the coin of choice most often, but any coin is possible. Also, the year can be significant. If it is the year when your loved one was born or died, or if it has a correlation to something you are worried about in your life (maybe you are worried about your son, and the coin you find is from the year of his birth), that is likely a sign from the other side that you aren't alone.

The doppelgänger spirit: This fascinating occurrence is when a spirit superimposes itself over a living person to give us the feeling of recognizing them. Spirits usually do this when we're in line or in a social situation. If you have never experienced this phenomenon, you may be surprised to learn how often others have. A person who is asking for a sign from her father might be walking down a busy street and pass by a person who looks just like her dad. When she turns around to get a better look, either that person is gone or, upon closer inspection, his appearance isn't what she has just seen. In my experience, spirits will often take the appearance of a similar form, overlaying themselves on that person to catch your attention. It's eerie, I know, but it's also quite comforting when you've been asking for a sign that a loved one is still around you.

Electricity: Electricity is a very popular way in which spirits send us signs, because of the energy connection and, I believe, because it is difficult for anyone to deny. When we cross over, we are in pure energy form, and we have the ability to blend with the electrical currents and manipulate the flow. This is why we see lights dim or switch off, see televisions turn on or off for no apparent reason, and hear phones ring with no physical caller on the other end. Yes, a lightbulb could just be old or there could be faulty wiring, but if the light goes out when you are seeking a sign, there is a pretty good chance it is a sign. My partner and I were watching television one night when the lights in the room — fairly new lights, in fact — continually flickered on and off. He was getting frustrated and exclaimed, "What the heck is going on?" I laughed and said, "You know *exactly* what's going on!" Once the lights stayed on for a while, we went about our business, only for them to go out *again*. "Oh, come on!" my partner cried. "What do you *want*?" This kind of thing is normal in the house of a psychic medium, and it's amusing how routine it has become for us.

Phones: I have heard many stories of a deceased loved one making someone's phone ring with their old name or number on the caller ID, and I have validated the spirit's identity in readings. This is similar to when my mom passed away. Though I never experienced it personally, several people living in the home that my mom had occupied had experiences of answering the landline phone and hearing her voice through a lot of static. Because they are communication devices and use electrical currents, phones have energy that spirits like to play with. (Also, you'll later read a wonderful story about a text message I unknowingly sent that turned out to be a sign for someone.)

License plates: Discussed briefly in my first book, the numbers or letters on license plates are another common method spirits like to use to get our attention. And it doesn't always have to be the license plate itself; it can be a car with a very personal message getting in front of you. For example, I have a friend who was, sadly, driving to his grandfather's funeral. On the highway, a semi cut him off in the left lane and wouldn't get out of his way. My friend was growing irritated that it wouldn't move — until he finally noticed an advertisement for Shriners Hospitals for Children on the back of the truck. He had never seen an ad for those hospitals on the back of a semi before. His grandfather had been a full-time volunteer at one of the hospitals for the last twenty years of his life.

"Name-calling": Hearing your loved one's name called out in a public space, seeing it where you wouldn't expect it, and hearing someone say a phrase your loved one commonly used while you are thinking of them are very common ways to receive signs. Yes, there will be people out there who have the same name as your deceased father; every time you hear his name will not be a sign. But you'll know it's a sign for you if you've recently been thinking of him, or if you feel an emotional response.

Music/sounds: Music is the rhythm of the cosmos. It has the power to move us on deep and meaningful levels. Because of the ability of music to resonate with our emotional states, spirits often love to communicate this way. A song may come on the radio at just the right moment to lift us up and remind us how the bond of love we shared with that person cannot be broken by their death. It could be a tune a loved one used to always sing to us or a track played at their funeral service. Whatever the meaning may be to us personally, it is their way of connecting with us from the other side to say, "Hey, I'm still here; don't worry about me." (In the next section you will read stories about music coming through to people as signs — I think you will find them quite fascinating.) Buzzing is another sign. Our human sense picks up on the very high level of vibration of the spirit world and interprets it as buzzing. Have you ever heard an intense buzzing sound in either ear for no apparent reason? When this happens, take note of what is going on around you. Trust that if you experience this sensation and start immediately thinking, for example, of a distant family member, and then you suddenly receive an email or text from them, this could have been a deceased loved one trying to connect the two of you. Spirits often intervene to try to bring people back together when it's for their higher good.

Dates: I find that my readings (which are scheduled by my assistant and orchestrated by spirits) are often randomly set for a date with significance to the client, such as a birthday or anniversary that pertains to a deceased loved one. I feel like my assistant is being guided to pick the perfect date on a subconscious level. It is also very common for someone looking for a sign to see, say, the digits 1114 in a phone number — and it later dawns on them that their loved one's birthday was on November 14. Skeptics who call that coincidence don't seem to think about the fact that there are 365 different days in a year among which to choose to schedule a reading. For *that* date to be the one that comes up in some way as you are hoping for a sign is pretty improbable, unless there is an outside force behind it, of course.

Numbers/time: Spirits love to communicate with us through numbers. My mom uses 143. That is a code for "I love you," which we started to use with each other a few months before her death when we both had pagers. I also had a website once when I was fifteen years old that was dedicated to the singer Jewel (I know, crazy fan). In the guest book, a message was signed 143. That message, I would learn, was from my mom. She was the one who left it and signed it 143 just before she passed. Now I see that number everywhere. It's such a random number to anyone else, but not me. Time is also a way signs are passed along. Many people, including me, believe that when they randomly see that the time is 11:11, it is a sign that angels are watching. When you realize that "11:11" is displayed on a clock for only two minutes each day, and you find yourself frequently seeing it, that can be very comforting and powerful.

Animals/bugs: Birds and other animals can be signs. In my first book, I talked about a woman who was annoyed by a bird that continually tapped on her windows. No matter what room the woman was in, the bird was out there. About that same time, she had scheduled a reading with me. Not knowing what she had been dealing with, I told her that her mother was coming through to me and that she was trying to tell me something about encounters with a bird. After my client acknowledged to me that she had been incessantly bothered by a bird tapping on her windows, her mother flashed an image of herself throwing her head back and laughing. It completely changed the daughter's perspective. Instead of hiring an exterminator to get rid of the bird, which she had been considering, she embraced its presence from that point forward. I also find that ladybugs are often a significant sign to people. Ladybugs are symbolic of enjoying life and living it to the fullest. Their gentle presence and beauty make them ideal signs to send a message from spirits that they want you to be happy in life doing what you love.

Of course, not everything we see or hear or experience is a sign from the other side. I have witnessed people in my group readings who are so grief-stricken by the loss of a loved one that they will try to "manufacture" a sign. I can't tell you how many times during an audience reading I will say something like "Is there someone here with a connection to a mother named Judy who died of an aneurysm?" and a person will raise her hand and enthusiastically shout, "Yes! My mother was Monica!" I mean, *really*? I understand that she so very much wants to hear from her mom, but there is no way to get "Monica" from "Judy."

Some people will do the same with numbers or time. If you believe that your sign from your loved one is seeing the time 3:21 and at 3:15 you sit and stare at the clock for six minutes, that's *not* a sign. It has to be something random, something spontaneous, something that happens without you forcing it. It is not a true sign or visitation if you are purposely putting yourself into a situation with a predictable outcome.

If your grandpa's lucky number was 75 and you travel daily on Interstate 75 in Florida to get to work, that doesn't mean your grandfather is sending you that sign every single day you see that number on the highway. Now, if you are on that highway thinking about your grandpa, who drove a Chevrolet, and you are passed by a '75 Chevy Nova, I'd say there's a pretty good chance *that* is a sign.

Another way to detect whether something is a sign is if you feel chills when it occurs. Getting chills or goose bumps is your soul's way of sending a signal to your body that what you just saw or heard came from your loved one. That doesn't mean something isn't a sign if you don't get those physical feelings; it's just more validation when you do experience them.

There are people so cynical that they will continually deny that a sign is a sign, chalking it up to "coincidence." I try to tell them to at least give the spirits a chance, to open their minds to the possibilities. Our feelings are our truth. When we tune in to them, we will better be able to understand them in a deep way, which will enable us to connect with the other side much more effectively, producing momentous experiences and tremendous healing.

I hope you are touched as you read about such experiences and healing in the following stories. Some of those involved are people who have had readings with me. Others I've never met but are friends of friends. While some names have been changed to protect identities, the stories are 100 percent true. Open your mind and enjoy!

Part III

TRUE
TESTIMONIES
OF THE
SPIRIT WORLD

6 Take Me Home, Country Roads

After receipt of a sign, one of the most fascinating and enjoyable discoveries that can be made is backtracking to see how it was orchestrated. Sometimes a sign is put right in front of us and we notice it right away, but oftentimes it can take a spirit hours, days, weeks, or longer to push a sign through to us. We don't recognize the actual process as it is unfolding, because we haven't seen its conclusion yet. But once the sign is received, we can realize, in retrospect, what the spirit went through to make it happen. This beautiful story about a man and his great-uncle helps us grasp the concept that spirits are always at work in our lives, even when we are not cognizant of it.

Anthony's great-uncle George passed away suddenly one fall morning at the age of eighty-seven. George was born and raised in the mountains of West Virginia and lived there his entire life. He was a hardworking family man who had been married to his wife, Marilyn, for sixty-nine years. Anthony didn't get to see George as often as he would have liked, given that they lived several hundred miles from each other, but when they did get together, usually during summer family reunions, they enjoyed each other's company very much.

Anthony found out that morning through a post on social media that his great-uncle had just been rushed to the hospital. George had evidently been sitting outside on the porch when he started to feel sick. Anthony called his mother (George's niece) and told her what he had read. When she phoned Marilyn to find out how George was doing, she was told that he had just died. Less than two hours passed from the time George had yelled for Marilyn to call an ambulance to his death. It happened that quickly.

Anthony went to work that day, though his thoughts were focused on his great-uncle.

"He had that deep West Virginia drawl when he spoke," Anthony said. "I loved to listen to him tell stories. As a hobby after he retired, he taught himself how to make wine, and he went all in with it. He had a lot of land, so he grew grapes and blackberries. He bought instruction manuals on how to turn them into wine. He purchased all the equipment he needed to do it. He even found a local bottle supplier. It was quite a one-man operation he had. He'd make so much wine that he'd run out of room to store it, so he'd have wine parties with his friends on the weekends just to get rid of some of it. Each time I saw him, he'd give me a few bottles. That blackberry wine was some of the best I'd ever tasted."

What Anthony found funny as he thought about George

that day was that he couldn't get a particular song out of his head.

"One year we'd had a family reunion at a park near George's house. One of my relatives had brought a cassette player and a tape with just one song on it: John Denver's 'Take Me Home, Country Roads.' For those who aren't familiar with it, it became the state song of West Virginia. The chorus begins 'Country roads, take me home, to the place I belong, West Virginia....' One of my great-aunts played the song over and over and over during the reunion, driving some of my relatives crazy. I guess that memory, along with the fact that George was a true West Virginian, put that song in my head as I reminisced about him. Fortunately, I like John Denver and that song, so I was fine with it playing on a loop in my mind."

Fast-forward to that evening. Anthony and his wife are in a monthly bowling league. They usually get to the alley for each match at about seven o'clock. They have fifteen minutes to warm up, and then the games begin. They bowl three games with their two teammates and four opponents. Sometimes they are finished by nine, other times by nine thirty, but never later than that. On this night, though, anything that *could* go wrong with the lanes did.

"Our first game started late because, after warm-ups, the power on our two lanes shut down. There were fifty-something lanes in that place, and ours were the only ones not working. Then, at least twice that first game, we had to go to the desk to ask them to manually adjust the scores because the electronic scoring wasn't working properly. A little bit later, after two people had bowled, neither of their balls came back. When an employee finally arrived after several minutes to fix the issue, she had to unscrew part of the floor near the ball return to see what was jamming it. She reached in and pulled out an actual pin that had fallen into the ball return. I've been bowling for thirty years, and I'd never seen that happen before. It was as if our lanes were haunted. It was a very strange night, to say the least."

By the time they'd completed the final frame of their third and last game, most of the bowling alley was empty. It was pushing ten o'clock.

"We had never been there that late," Anthony said. "Not even close. Nearly three hours to bowl three games was unheard of. I'd never encountered so many problems on two lanes side by side."

Anthony and his wife changed their shoes, packed up their stuff, and finally headed out. When they got to their car, he tossed his bag into the backseat before sliding behind the wheel.

"We'd had an enjoyable evening with our friends, and we really didn't have a reason to rush home other than we had to work the next day, but my wife and I and everyone else were ready to get out of there after all the electronic and mechanical problems. Bowling is fun, but when you have to keep starting and stopping all night, and when you expect to be finished closer to nine than ten, it wears on you a little bit."

When Anthony started the car, the radio came on. The station was tuned to the one he listened to 95 percent of the time. It played a lot of hit songs from the 1970s and 1980s. He was hoping to hear a good one that would lighten his mood a bit.

What he heard blew his mind.

Anthony threw his head back against the headrest, his mouth

hanging open in utter disbelief. "You've got to be kidding!" he exclaimed.

"What's wrong?" his wife asked.

Anthony paused for a moment, trying to keep his emotions in check. "Absolutely nothing," he said softly.

How could anything be wrong when the song playing on the radio at that moment was "Take Me Home, Country Roads"?

It wasn't just the song. It was *that* song...on *that* station... at *that* moment.

"Over the last twenty years, I have listened to that station at some point nearly every single day, usually in my car, and I can tell you without any doubt whatsoever that I had never heard that song on that station. In fact, I can't think of any John Denver song that station has ever played. That's not to say they've never played one, but you would have thought that an avid listener like me would have heard one before. I wouldn't have even considered calling them and requesting that song, because I never would have expected them to play it."

Anthony knew who was behind it.

"There was no question to me, as I reflected on the evening after hearing that song, that George was responsible for every-thing that happened. In all the years I'd been bowling, I'd never seen so many problems arise the way they did on those two lanes. I mean, seriously, a bowling pin goes through the ball return? How many people have ever witnessed that? And for those delays to not only last as long as they did, but to be timed just right so that I would get in my car during the brief three minutes and eight seconds that song lasts — it was just astonishing."

As you will read throughout all these firsthand accounts,

spirits work in different ways to get signs to their loved ones, sometimes even orchestrating elaborate plans. George obviously knew what was playing in Anthony's mind all day, and he decided to comfort his great-nephew in what he thought would be the most convincing and reassuring manner.

"If someone wants to claim that everything that happened that night was coincidental, then to each his own. But how many coincidences does it take for someone to admit that there could be something beyond this world that is responsible for what is happening around us? There were too many inexplicable occurrences that day, from morning to night and in perfect synchronicity, for me to believe that anything other than George himself was responsible. He did just about everything he could, short of making a visual appearance, to get my attention. When I went to bed that night and looked back on the entire day, from that morning when the song entered my mind to hearing it on the radio that evening, I realized what a beautiful journey George had taken me on. It is something that will stay in my heart forever."

7 The Color Heather

Receiving a sign from the other side at any time is a beautiful experience, but there may be nothing more beautiful than receiving one so vivid and of such extraordinary significance as one man did when it was the furthest thing from his mind.

Jeff and Heather McManamy were never religious. They didn't attend church. They didn't necessarily believe in God. But they did believe in something.

"I never could discount the power of a person's soul," Jeff said. "That's just too much energy to be gone in the blink of an eye."

But Jeff never actively looked for signs or expected his wife to provide him any after she died. That didn't stop her, though, from sending him one so convincing that he knew immediately that her soul was still with him.

A vivacious woman whose charm and wit endeared her even to strangers, Heather was thirty-three when she was diagnosed with stage IV metastatic breast cancer. The worst part of her grim prognosis was knowing she would miss seeing her four-year-old daughter, Brianna, grow up. She became an internet sensation when she shared on social media that she had bought greeting cards for every future special occasion of Brianna's life — from first days of school to her retirement — for Jeff to give to Brianna after Heather was gone. Entreating everyone who followed her journey to live each day as if it were their final one, Heather walked the walk by turning in the manuscript for her memoir, *Cards for Brianna*, one day before her death. She passed away at the age of thirty-six. Her book was published four months later, and in multiple languages.

Soon after the book was released, Jeff decided it was time to start a new chapter in his and Brianna's lives.

"I decided to sell our house," he said. "I felt like all those recent years of cancer had trumped the good memories we'd had there. But I struggled a lot with the decision. It was the first house we'd bought together. It was the only home Bri had known. Did leaving there mean that we were leaving Heather? I knew it didn't, but it was a connection we'd had that I was about to break. I fretted over it for a long time, even after I made my decision."

Jeff made his new purchase in a new nearby subdivision. It was one of the last lots left, and the home was already under construction when he bought it. He met with the designer to approve everything the builder intended to do inside the home, including appliances, flooring, and colors.

"When I got there, they had the paint swatches out for the walls and the trim," Jeff said. "It all pretty much looked white to me, but the trim was a slightly different shade of white."

Of course, nothing in the paint world is referred to as a different shade of something else. Every color has a name.

"The color for the trim was spelled out right there in front of me," Jeff said. "It was 'Heather.' The color was actually called *heather*. I said, 'Oh my God.' The designer asked if there was a problem. I was so stunned that I wasn't sure I'd be able to explain, so I simply said, 'No. Everything is perfect.'"

Jeff took a picture of the color with its label and called his mom the second his meeting was finished. "She and everyone else I told said that was Heather letting me know that I'd done the right thing and that I did a good job picking that house," Jeff said. "I knew without a doubt it was a sign that she was okay with my decision."

This sign led Jeff to recall the first few weeks after Heather's death, when lightbulbs throughout the house had gone out. "I'm not talking like one or two bulbs. It was probably ten bulbs in three weeks," he said. "We'd never had an issue before, and now, suddenly, it seemed like every single one was going out."

He didn't attribute it to Heather at the time. Now, after the incident with the designer, he did.

"I believe Heather tried to get my attention with the light-bulbs, but it didn't work," he said. "So, she took it up a notch with the trim color. When I put the two signs together, there really is no explanation other than that Heather was behind it all. It reaffirms for me that she is not gone. Even though she died, and even though we moved, her energy is still with us, and it always will be."

8 The Laughing Hummingbird

Sometimes spirits will send us signs that they think we will recognize as such, but instead we perceive them as something completely different — a coincidence, a logical part of our everyday life, or even an annoyance. This is why it is so important for us to always keep our minds open to everything around us. What may appear to be nothing noteworthy could be life changing if we view it in a different light.

Take the story of Mary, who lives in Nevada and enjoys immersing herself in nature. The scenery, the fresh-air smell, the wildlife — it all brings her a sense of love and peace. She even built a greenhouse in her backyard. Many of the hours in her day are filled taking care of the various flowers and plants she has nurtured over the years.

Mary's mother lived in nearby California, and Mary often traveled there, where they gardened together, until her mother's death in 2006.

"She was a highly creative woman," Mary said. "She would get very upset with herself if she couldn't figure out how to do everything on her own, whether it was developing an underground watering system on timers for her many plants, or hand-making our dad's silk suits and all our clothes when we were kids. She was a very determined person, with a wonderful sense of humor and a happy and boisterous laugh."

About five years after her mom died, Mary's sister in California had scheduled a phone reading with me. Up to that point, I had no idea who Mary was. Her sister was the first in the family to have a reading.

Each day, starting about two weeks prior to her sister's reading, Mary would get a visitor in the greenhouse. An unwelcome one, of sorts.

"I would open the doors each morning and leave them open, and what appeared to be the same hummingbird would fly in day after day and hover around some purple lanterns I had hanging," Mary said. "The bird did the same thing every time. It would fly around the lanterns, then rest on a beam and chirp at me as it bobbed up and down and flapped its wings. I would try to shoo it out, but it wouldn't go. It was like it was laughing at me."

The fact that this bird had the same routine every single day, including refusing to fly away when Mary tried to make it leave, could have come across as a sign to her if she had considered that possibility. But she simply saw it as a wild bird with not a lot of smarts.

When Mary's sister had her reading with me, her mother was coming through very clearly. "She's showing me a hummingbird," I said.

"A hummingbird?" Mary's sister had no idea what I was

talking about. She couldn't recall the last time she'd even seen a hummingbird.

"Do you have a sister? She's telling me you need to call your sister," I said. "I am also sensing a booming laugh from her." These impressions were very random, which is how messages are often presented to me.

A hummingbird, followed by an order to call her sister, followed by a booming laugh? Mary's sister was confused. She knew, of course, about her mother's laugh, but what did a hummingbird and her sister have to do with it?

Of course, none of it made sense to me, either. As the messenger, I rely on those I'm reading for to piece together what the spirits are transmitting to me. On the surface, I could understand why she was confused, but I always trust what the spirits are telling me. I knew there was some logic to this. It was going to be up to Mary's sister to figure that out over time.

"I would just call your sister," I said. "Your mom seems insistent that you do that."

So, after the reading, she made the call. "Mary, I had my reading with the medium Bill and Mom came through, but some of it didn't make any sense to me," she confessed. "He said Mom was showing him a hummingbird, and she was laughing."

Mary screamed. She actually *screamed*.

Once she calmed down, she told her sister the story of the hummingbird, and as they talked they even recalled that their mom's favorite color was purple, which would explain why the bird was so infatuated with the lanterns.

"It was unbelievable," Mary said. And you can imagine how happy she was when the bird returned to the greenhouse the day after the reading.

"I called my sister and told her it was back," Mary explained. "We laughed and cried together."

The hummingbird was no longer just a hummingbird. Mary's eyes had been opened to an entirely new world.

"I talked to it, and it became very comfortable with me," she said. "It let me get very close to it, to the point that it almost hopped into my hand.

"I didn't understand at first why Mom would have sent a hummingbird — they had no direct significance in either of our lives when she was alive. But I guess since we did do a lot of gardening together, and since hummingbirds and flowers go hand in hand, she thought that would be a good way to get my attention and let me know she was with me."

One thing to note about how signs like this work is that the hummingbird was not actually Mary's mother. It was a sign *sent* by her mother. She chose what she thought would be the best method to reach her daughter, to let her know that she was watching over her. Since she knew her daughter was always in the greenhouse, the hummingbird probably seemed like a logical choice.

9 "Oh, That Sly Grin..."

I t has been my experience that spirits tend to like the element of surprise, probably because springing signs upon us can have more weight of conviction. While it is vital that you always be open to and aware of potential signs around you, most of them will occur when you least expect them and oftentimes in ways you might have never imagined. Strike a balance...live your life, but also remember in the back of your mind that the other side is always at work.

One person who did just that was Jennifer. She had worked with a woman named Rosie for many years, and the two had become very good friends. After they went their separate ways professionally, they would still try to get together every year or so. One summer they and their families spent a weekend camping together in Illinois. Rosie had had recent health issues and was diagnosed with fibromyalgia. While it certainly caused her some hardship, she seemed to be managing it well on their camping trip.

About eight months later, however, Rosie called Jennifer with some horrible news.

"It was the death call," Jennifer said. "Rosie told me she had been misdiagnosed. It wasn't fibromyalgia at all. It was bone cancer. I didn't know what to say. I cried. We cried. They didn't know how long she had, but the cancer had obviously been spreading for a while. She was already in stage IV and probably didn't have a lot of time left. She was living in Texas when she called, but she said she was going to try to get to Illinois to see me and other friends sometime in the next couple of months."

A few weeks later, Jennifer had to travel overseas for business. It was then that she received word that Rosie had passed away.

"I was devastated," Jennifer said. "On top of that, I wasn't able to go to her service because I was out of the country. I felt horrible. It all happened so quickly."

About seven months after Rosie had died, Jennifer, her husband, their two children, and some of their relatives were on a Disney cruise traveling to the US Virgin Islands. "We were standing in line waiting to have our picture taken with the ship's captain," Jennifer said. "It was right before dinner. The kids were hungry and cranky. I was hungry, too, and ready to relax after a fun but long day. My husband took the kids across the way to look out a porthole to keep them entertained while I leaned against a wall, holding our place in line for the photo."

Though she had thought about Rosie a lot since her death, Jennifer admits she wasn't thinking about her while standing in line. That is why what happened next was all the more fascinating.

"A woman appeared from around the corner. She was wearing a simple but gorgeous navy-blue gown. It was full-length with a V-neck in the front and sheer sleeves. She had a dazzling necklace and earrings. Her hair was short, vibrant, and red. And that grin. Oh, that sly grin she had. It was Rosie to a tee. Even the shape of her body and the way she walked. It was uncanny. That is why I remember every detail about her so well. I was staring right at Rosie."

From the second this woman and Jennifer saw each other, their eyes remained locked.

"We never broke eye contact," Jennifer said. "It probably lasted less than ten seconds, but it felt like ten minutes. Even as she continued to walk by and head toward the dining area, she turned her head and stayed focused on me. Neither of us said a word. We said it all with our eyes. I was overcome with chills. I watched her all the way until she rounded the corner and was out of sight. I wanted to chase after her, but I don't know what I would have said or how I would have reacted. Seconds later, my husband ran back to me with the kids."

"Did you just see that?" he said to Jennifer.

She had a witness, and she was grateful for it. "Not that I needed one, because I knew what I had seen, but when my husband said he had seen her, too, I broke down and cried right there in line," she said. "Not exactly the thing to do when you are about to have a picture taken with the captain, but I had no control over it. This woman was Rosie, spot-on. As astonished as I was to have seen her and as emotional as I was at that moment, it also brought me such peace."

For the rest of the cruise, Jennifer continually looked for the woman. "At dinner, in the hallways, by the pool. And believe me, I was looking nonstop. But I never saw her again."

I've found that creating a doppelgänger is not as common as some of the other ways that spirits will send signs, but when this method is used, every detail will stick with you. Especially in a case such as this one, in which the woman made and held eye contact with Jennifer.

"I had heard of people saying they had seen someone who looked like someone they knew who had died, but it had never happened to me before," Jennifer said. "Now I know it can really happen. There was no question in my mind that that was Rosie's signal to me that she was in a good place.

"And I can assure you that if that's the only sign I get from anyone in my lifetime, I'm good."

10 The Power of Two Strands of Tinsel

This next story may be a bit difficult to read, given the nature of the abuse Dorothy endured. I have tried not to get too detailed or graphic. However, I think it is important to understand just how dark a place Dorothy was in and how, despite that, spirits can still bring tremendous comfort, even years after their passing, with a simple but poignant sign.

Dorothy was in an abusive marriage. It was unlike anything I had personally ever heard. Her husband abused her emotionally, physically, and financially. He cut her off from her friends and family. He would drag their crying daughter upstairs with him and refuse to let Dorothy come up to console her. He'd repeatedly threaten to take their child out of the country and to his native land. This went on for more than a decade. Dorothy had wanted out for a long time, but as those who have been in abusive relationships know, that is far easier said than done.

Growing up, long before she had ever met her husband, Dorothy had been very close to her paternal grandmother. Her grandma died of Alzheimer's when Dorothy was seventeen, but she never left Dorothy's mind and heart.

"I always talked to her after she died, always," Dorothy said. "Once I was in that abusive relationship with my husband, talking to her was one way I could find a sliver of comfort and hope."

Just prior to Christmas one year, when her daughter was four years old, Dorothy wanted to decorate their tree with her.

"My husband was angry with me, so he took our daughter upstairs and refused to let her come down to help me. As I started to decorate the tree myself, I came across my grandma's antique ornaments that she had given me. There were five of them. I cried when I pulled them out of the box. I began to talk to my grandma out loud through the tears, telling her how much I missed her, how much Christmas reminded me of her, how much I wanted to hear from her, and how I really needed her help getting out of my marriage. It had been about ten years since she had died, but I never lost faith that she was still with me. I know I was throwing a lot at her at that moment, but I was desperate. The abuse was daily, and in many forms. As much as I wanted to just take my daughter and run away, I was terrified that he would hunt us down and kill us both."

Dorothy displayed her grandma's ornaments prominently in the front and center of the tree, but she was bothered by something that was missing — tinsel. Dorothy had never used it on her own tree before, but tinsel had been her grandma's thing.

"It would take my grandma hours to decorate her tree every year because she would put so much tinsel on it, one strand at a time. She was very precise about where it was placed. One piece couldn't cross over another. It couldn't be clumped together. That precision is why she always had the most beautiful tree. I had been thinking the whole week prior that I needed to get some for my tree, and I had gone to a few stores looking for it, but they were all sold out."

When Dorothy had made her tree look the best that a tinsel-less tree possibly could, and after her husband and daughter were both asleep, she went upstairs to bed. The next morning she woke up before sunrise, went downstairs, and turned on the tree's lights. She noticed the lights reflecting off something shiny near one of the ornaments.

"I put my hand over my mouth; I was frozen from head to toe," Dorothy said. "Lying over the top of one of the ornaments Grandma had given me were two strands of tinsel. They weren't crossed or clumped. They were each resting vertically and perfectly straight over the ornament, not touching each other, just like she would have hung them."

Dorothy had never had a single piece of tinsel in her house. Even if there had been a couple of remnants in the boxes that held her grandma's ornaments, there certainly hadn't been any on that ornament when she hung it the night before.

"Nobody in the house could have done it overnight," said Dorothy. "Not only did we not have any, but my daughter was too short to reach that ornament, and there is no way my husband would have done it."

Dorothy began that morning the way she had ended her previous evening — crying. But the tears now had new meaning.

"There was no question that my grandma was with me that previous night, that she had heard my pleas and recognized the pain I was going through. Maybe she had sent me signs in the past and I just didn't notice them. But there was no missing or denying this one. She made certain of that."

After Christmas, as she was taking down the tree, Dorothy carefully removed the two strands of tinsel and placed them in their own box.

"That tinsel was, is, and always will be my hope. I grew up with an aunt who was psychic and a mother who was Catholic. I was raised to pray, not just to God but to my deceased relatives. I have always found comfort in prayer, which is what I was doing that evening. But to physically see an answer to my prayer the next morning in the midst of everything horrible I was going through — all I could say was 'Yes! Thank you, Grandma!'"

Life did not immediately get better for Dorothy, but that tinsel gave her enough hope at just the right time for her to work toward the peace she so desired and deserved.

"You become very isolated when you are going through such trauma," she said. "That is why I turned to my grandma. She became my lifeline. She heard me, and I knew she was going to help me get out of this. She would become my rock through it all. It would take another six or seven years to get out, but I finally did. He is now my ex-husband. I have no doubt that my grandma helped save me from an abusive marriage."

11 A Spirit's Road Rage

Some people take longer than others to figure out what they want to do in terms of a career. I was certainly an example of that. I took some classes at a community college, then went to school to be an opera singer, then upon graduation decided to put my psychic medium skills to use instead. Elizabeth Collins wasn't sure what she wanted to do, either, but what caused her to finally arrive at the decision she made was quite intriguing.

Elizabeth knew she wanted to do one of two things in the medical field: become a nurse practitioner or a physician's assistant. A nurse practitioner is an advanced registered nurse who can perform duties similar to a physician. A physician's assistant is similar to a nurse practitioner but can perform duties only under the supervision of a physician.

Elizabeth came to me one day for a reading, hoping I could help her figure out what to do.

"I was in an associate's degree program in the arts and was graduating in a few months. After that, I was going to continue my education to become a nurse practitioner or physician's assistant, so I had to make up my mind very soon about what I was going to do," Elizabeth said.

"There were pros and cons to both careers. Every time I would decide on one, I'd change my mind to the other. I'd wasted a lot of time and money with my indecisiveness, so I went to Bill for some guidance."

During Elizabeth's reading with me, no particular spirit came through. Most people set up readings hoping to connect with someone specific on the other side. In Elizabeth's case, she had nobody in mind she was looking to connect with. She just wanted an answer to her dilemma no matter how it came about — and an answer is exactly what she got, albeit a strange one.

Just when I think I've received every kind of message that I could from the other side, a new one always pops up. I told Elizabeth that she would be distracted by a car and that it would give her the answer.

"I thought, *Are you kidding me? What does that mean?* Bill said it could be, for example, that I would be passing a really nice car that catches my eye, and I would then happen to notice a billboard in the background that would reveal my answer — something like that. It seemed like a very odd way to get an answer to something so important in my life, but Bill was adamant that this was what was coming through to him, so I trusted him."

Days and weeks went by after her reading; Elizabeth still didn't have her answer. I had never told her when she would get it, and I usually can't in any reading. Spirits are in a place where time doesn't exist, so we often have to be patient with them, maybe for longer than we'd like.

It is important to note here that during readings, spirits

do not always provide me with every bit of information they possibly can, because they don't want me to reveal all the steps or answers. That would negate the need for our own intuition. What spirits will usually do is provide unique clues to motivate the client to tap into their own intuition and open their mind. Once that is established, the answers will come in clearly and at the perfect time.

For Elizabeth, getting the answer she sought took a few months. It happened one day when she was heading to the store during her lunch break from school to purchase her cap and gown for graduation. She was driving through Fort Worth in the right lane on an interstate, preparing to get off at the next exit.

"All of a sudden, this car came flying up my left side at a ridiculous speed and cut to the right, directly in front of me. He came so close to hitting me that I swerved to the right onto the shoulder and ultimately into the grass. Fortunately, I was able to maintain control of the car without stopping and get back on the road. But boy, was I ticked!"

Elizabeth pushed the pedal to the floor, spewing several expletives along the way, as she caught up to and got right on the tail of the car. She was looking at the license-plate number when she noticed the frame around the plate.

"It said: 'I love being an NP' — a nurse practitioner," she said.

And as if that wasn't convincing enough, she noticed the car itself.

"It was a black Camaro. For as long as I had been driving, that had always been my dream car. I had told myself that one day, when I could afford it, I would buy myself a black Camaro.

"I couldn't believe it," she continued. "My cussing instantly turned into a 'Wow!' I backed off the bumper of the Camaro and had a completely new perspective. I instantly recalled my meeting with Bill and how he had said a distraction from a car would reveal my answer as to what direction I should take with regard to my career. Here I was, on my way to get my cap and gown, and I got cut off and run off the road by my dream car with a plate frame about loving being an NP. There was nothing subtle about this. The career decision I needed to make had literally been put right in front of my face."

And she wasted no time acting upon it. "When I got to school later that day, I went right to the office to put in my application for nursing school. I'd gone back and forth so many times trying to decide, but not this time; I didn't give it another thought. I was among three hundred people who would apply for just forty openings, and I was one they would ultimately select."

While the story could have ended there with all the conviction she needed, Elizabeth would receive one more validation that she had made the right decision.

She was in her car again one day, on the interstate in Fort Worth, in the right lane — fortunately, she didn't get cut off this time. Her dad had just died of cancer, and she had missed her first week of nursing school as a result. Her father had been very proud of her for sticking with her schooling and finally making the decision to be an NP. But losing him right when she was supposed to start her studies was very difficult. As she exited the highway to go to her first day of class, there was a homeless man standing on the corner.

"For two years I'd been getting off at this exit nearly every day, and I had never seen a homeless person standing there. I'd seen them in other areas, and I am always that person who holds up traffic to scrounge together whatever money I can find to give to them. But this was a very rare moment in which I just didn't want to do it. I was tired. I was depressed. I'd just lost the person closest to me, and I was not in the mood to interact with anybody."

But her mind was changed as soon as she drove past the man and got a good look at him.

"He was big like my dad, but it was his eyes that struck me. They were just like my dad's, which were unique. Big, and blue, but so blue that they appeared almost crystal clear. I don't know how else to describe them, but I couldn't recall ever seeing anyone with eyes like my dad had."

Elizabeth was so taken with the man that, after turning at the light, she pulled over, grabbed a few dollar bills from her center console, and then turned her car around to drive back and give him the money.

"He leaned down to my window and smiled and said, 'I knew you'd come back.' I said, 'You did?' As I handed him the money, he replied, 'Yes, I did. And don't worry — everything is going to be okay.' A homeless man was telling me that he knew I'd be back and that everything was going to be okay? Normally, I'd wonder how he could know and what that meant, but in my heart, I was staring right into the soul of my dad. I knew how this man knew and what he meant. It was exactly the validation I needed that I'd made the right career choice, and that even without my dad being physically with me, he was still with me in spirit."

Elizabeth is still in school today and well on her way to becoming an NP. That was the only time she would see that man or anyone else asking for money at that exit.

After she becomes an NP and saves some money, she knows how she will spend it. "I'm going to get that Camaro," she said. "I didn't see that car cutting me off as just a sign that I was supposed to become an NP. It was also a sign that I am definitely supposed to buy myself that car!"

12 That Hawk, and More Hawks

This is a story about Christine and her father. It shows the power of animals to be messengers from the other side, how spirits use the wisdom and symbolism of animals to convey signs to us, and how embracing animals as signs can bring peace and happiness into our lives.

Nearly a decade ago, Christine's father had been diagnosed with a very aggressive form of cancer. He flew from his home in New York to Southern California to live with Christine while he received treatment. He was with his daughter for five months before he passed away.

"When they came to take his body away from my home, there was a lot going on. A lot of family and friends had gathered with us, and it was, of course, a very emotional time for everyone," Christine said. "As we were all gathered outside at one point that day, a few of us spotted a huge hawk flying above our house. We noticed it because in all the years we had lived there, we had never seen a single hawk. Every one of us saw it soaring above without pointing it out to each other. We were mesmerized by its beauty. Dad had been in a lot of pain and had been asking to die every night for weeks. He was ready to go and begin his next life. I couldn't help but wonder if this was a sign from him."

Christine felt she had found the answer to that in the days that followed. Every morning for the next month, she said a red-tailed hawk would land on a tree in her backyard and be in no rush to leave.

"It was a big pine tree. The hawk would land there at almost the same time each day and stay for several hours. I could clearly see it from my kitchen window. I didn't even have to search for it. I would just look out my window and there it would be on the same branch. It was bizarre how long it would stay there, and that it would always land right where I could see it."

After that month, when the hawk no longer landed in the tree each day, Christine began noticing hawks wherever she went.

"They were everywhere," she said. "I would see them when I went on bike rides. I would see them in Toronto and Montreal when I would travel to Canada for work. And I know it sounds crazy, but it seemed like anytime I would talk to my dad in spirit, a hawk would appear, no matter where I was."

Some people truly did think she was crazy. "I would tell people these stories, and they'd say 'Really?' Not with a tone like they found it fascinating, but as though they didn't necessarily believe me. A perfect example is one time when I was on my way to a hotel with a friend while we were vacationing in Cabo San Lucas, Mexico. She was one who had been skeptical of my hawk stories. While we were in the cab, I was talking about my dad. She was listening to me and looking out the window when suddenly she exclaimed, 'Christine! Look!' There was a hawk flying right beside us. She believes me now."

For her part, Christine believes so much in the appearance of the hawk as a sign from her dad that it has physically become part of who she is.

"Never in my life had I ever thought about getting a tattoo, but about a month ago I decided to get one of a hawk on my right wrist to keep my dad's spirit right in front of me every day. I also framed a picture I'd taken of that hawk that had been landing on my pine tree. It sits in my living room."

So, what was the significance of a hawk before her dad died?

"There was none at all," she said. "Like I said, I had never even seen a hawk where we lived. And I don't think hawks had any significance in my dad's life. It was just a feeling I had, that we all had, as soon as we looked toward the sky and saw the hawk that day he died. There was a real internal, spiritual connection. It brought me comfort then, and it continues to bring me comfort today."

Christine's story is a very good example of why we need to keep our minds open to any possible sign. Most people look for signs that would relate to themselves or to the person who died. And while I would say that often that's how spirits will communicate, it won't always be the case. Their number-one goal is to get our attention however they can. Christine's dad obviously saw a chance for the hawk to mean something to his daughter, at that moment and beyond. Had this sign not worked, he might have tried something else later. But it *did* work, because of Christine's openness to all possibilities.

13 More Than Just a Dream

When we're awake, numerous distractions — such as gadgets, health concerns, work issues, or family worries — gobble up our attention and could prevent us from recognizing a sign that's right in front of us. But when we sleep, those distractions tend to slip away as we enter our unconscious world, making it an ideal time for spirits to communicate with us. Yes, some dreams can be downright weird and have no meaning to us, but many of them contain significant messages from the other side.

Mike and Phyllis were high school sweethearts in the early 1980s and lived a fairy-tale romance for three years. They were best friends, loved each other with every ounce of energy that two teenagers could, and talked openly and extensively about their future together. There was no question in their minds, or in the minds of their friends and families, that they were going to be together forever. If there were ever a perfect love story, this was it.

"We were going to graduate from high school, continue

dating through college, and get married in our midtwenties," Phyllis said. "We had it all planned out."

But those plans shockingly unraveled during their senior year of high school.

"Mike got heavily involved in drinking and drugs, to the point of addiction," Phyllis said. "I kept giving him chances to change, but he wouldn't. He was no longer the same wonderful guy I'd fallen in love with. I knew he still loved me, but he had a serious problem that he couldn't overcome. I finally had to break up with him."

Mike continually begged Phyllis for another chance, and, after a year apart, she finally gave in. The two reconciled when he convinced her he was a changed man. "Things will be different," he assured her. They lasted four more months together.

"He tried in the beginning, but the addiction consumed him," Phyllis said. "We were just nineteen years old, and the path he was on was really bad. I mean, *really* bad. I could see he was not going to live a long life. It broke my heart, but I just couldn't do it anymore."

While Phyllis was certain she was done with Mike, he still wasn't convinced that it was over. Again and again he begged her to take him back. He called her. He showed up unexpectedly at her home. He appeared unannounced at her work.

"I had to keep pushing him away, figuratively and literally," she said.

Six months after their second breakup, with Mike still hounding her, Phyllis started dating a wonderful man who brought her much happiness, a police officer named Fred.

"I knew then that I couldn't have Mike in my life in any way, not even as a friend," she said. "He didn't like that, and he wouldn't take no for an answer. He continued to haunt me for another year or two."

Phyllis stayed true to Fred, and Mike finally backed off as he got deeper into drugs and his life continued in a downward spiral. After those couple of years, he would never contact Phyllis again.

Well, just not while he was *alive*.

Jump ahead more than a decade to one early morning in 1996. Phyllis and Fred had been happily married for several years. Fred was the love of her life. Mike was nothing more than a piece of her past. She hadn't seen him or heard anything about him for years. But on this particular day at about 6 AM, at the tail end of what had been a very peaceful night's sleep, Phyllis awoke gasping for air. Her body was trembling. She was in a severe panic. It was all enough to wake a startled Fred, who tried to calm her down as he asked her what was wrong.

"I'd had a dream about Mike. He wasn't doing or saying anything. He was…he was just there. The dream didn't last more than ten seconds, but I was left with a very powerful feeling that he was gone, that he had died. I hadn't seen him in so long and didn't know what he was doing with his life, but I knew in my heart he had passed. What really blew my mind was that I instantly recalled having a vision when I was nineteen years old that Mike would die from drug abuse when he was thirty-two. I realized he was thirty-two now. I couldn't believe any of this."

She shared the dream with Fred, who did exactly what she needed him to do: he listened. "I knew I had told Fred years earlier about the vision I'd had when I was nineteen. Fred remembered that conversation, and he was shaken that I was so certain Mike was dead."

Phyllis calmed herself enough to get out of bed to get ready for work. "But I couldn't stop thinking about the dream," she said. "I got to work and told all my coworkers about it. I also called and told my mother about it. She had always been my greatest teacher in life and had taught me to trust my instincts. I then called Fred to ask him if he would be okay with me calling Mike's parents after work. Having witnessed what an impact this dream had had on me, he had no problem with it. He knew how much Mike's parents loved me when Mike and I were dating, and I loved them. Mike's father even helped me through some difficult times when I was dealing with my own alcoholic father. I hadn't talked to them in five years, but they had been like parents to me during my teens. I needed to know if something happened. I needed to know if the feeling I had was real."

The dream was just the beginning of a string of profound events that would lead Phyllis to her answer.

"I had gone out for lunch to my mother's home and was on my way back to work when I came to a stoplight. A man who looked very familiar was crossing the street right in front of me. It took me a second... I just couldn't believe it."

The man was Mike's father.

"My nerves kicked in like they had when I woke up from that dream. I didn't know what was happening. How in the world was I seeing his dad for the first time in so many years just hours after having that dream?"

When the light turned green, Phyllis slammed her foot on the gas pedal and rushed back to work to tell her coworkers what had happened. She was frazzled, and she didn't know how she was going to be able to wait until after work to call Mike's parents, as she had planned. But she had no choice. Phyllis worked in a very fast-paced dermatology office, and there was no way she was going to make this call from work, knowing how emotional it would be if the dream were true.

Considering what would happen just minutes later, maybe Mike knew her predicament.

"The private work line rang and I answered it. The voice on the other end said, 'May I please speak to Felicea?' That was the nickname Mike's parents had given me, since they were French Canadian. I knew it was Mike's mother. I knew the voice. My heart was racing, and so was my mouth. 'Janet?' I said. 'This is Phyllis! Are you okay? Is Mike okay? I had this dream and was going to call you later. I just saw George crossing the street. What's wrong?'"

Phyllis's gut instinct about the dream was accurate. "Janet's voice became choked with tears," Phyllis said. "Not only was he dead, but she said she'd also had a dream that morning in which Mike told her not to forget to tell me he had died. The parallel was truly divine intervention. He had visited both of us that morning."

Janet told Phyllis they had buried him a week and a half earlier. "She said she was so sorry that she didn't call me sooner, but she hadn't wanted to interrupt my life."

With that, Phyllis told Janet that she would very much like to see her that week. A few days later, the two most important women in Mike's life greeted each other at Janet's door with a long and warm embrace, and a lot of tears.

"Mike orchestrated that meeting," Phyllis said. "I have a dream that he's dead, and Janet has a dream that she's supposed to call me to tell me that he just died, all after thirteen years? There is nothing coincidental about that."

Janet showed Phyllis Mike's bedroom, the same room he'd had when they were dating.

"I didn't even recognize it," she said. "There were a lot of religious artifacts and some really odd things. It had a gothic feel to it. His mom said he died in the house from an overdose. Because of the drugs, he'd had schizophrenia, AIDS, and hepatitis. What really hit me was that I knew when we were nineteen that his life was going to end like this when he was thirty-two. My inner voice then was so strong. I loved him so much, but he couldn't escape his addiction. His dad had even told me I should leave him because he knew Mike wasn't going to change. That's how clear this was to all of us."

Why does Phyllis believe Mike triggered these events she experienced, from the dream to the meeting with his mom?

"I was still his girl in his mind. Janet said he never had another girlfriend after me. I think he wanted me to know that he was in a better place, and I did sense that after going to his house and talking to his mom. He was at peace, no longer tormented by the drugs."

Phyllis said her dream and everything else that happened that day had a significant impact on her life going forward.

"My vision at nineteen years old, my dream, Janet's dream, Mike's father crossing the street in front of me, Janet calling me at work — it was one unbelievable event after another. I have never been religious or gone to church, but I have always had an inner voice I've listened to, which is the voice that told me to leave Mike when I did, and which I also know had something to do with my dream. I don't know what's out there, whether it's some sort of force or universal energy or God. But do I believe, after what I experienced that day, that we go somewhere after this life? I absolutely do."

Pay close attention to your dreams. Sometimes they will be as vivid and memorable as the ones Phyllis and Janet had, but other times you might forget them moments after you wake up. Write them down immediately so that you can recall them and analyze them later, and maybe even connect them to other dreams you've had or will have in the future. A dream can often be more than just a dream, especially when you are looking for a sign.

14 "Hey, Baby Girl…"

Think about how good it feels to be invited to something. An invitation is a welcome mat, a way of saying, "I would like you to enter into my life in this capacity," be it for a celebration of some sort or a simple visit. No doubt spirits will try to contact you if they want to, but if you invite them to contact you, the chances are much greater that they will, because they know for certain that you are open to their presence. Rose's story is an ideal example of that.

Rose works from home for a dentist doing computer data entry. She had just finished cutting the grass one summer day and had come inside to do some paperwork for her boss before showering. "It was already evening," Rose said. "I turned on my computer and the nearby lamp. Then I said out loud, 'Hey, baby girl, how are you doing?'"

Her "baby girl" was her youngest child, Madison. They called her Madi. She had died a few weeks earlier at the age of twenty. Madi had been born with severe disabilities that included neuromuscular damage. When she had been able to talk and had some movement in her body, which was until about her teenage years, she loved to sing, dance, float in water, and even ride horses. When she lost her voice and mobility, she enjoyed everything audiovisual, including listening to music, watching television, and having books read to her. She had three siblings — Charity, Jorge, and Christopher — who treated her no differently than they treated each other. They included her in whatever activities they did, teased her, and made her laugh. Madi was a very loving and happy girl who enjoyed the life she'd been given.

As any parent who has suffered the loss of a child will tell you, there is no greater pain. Since Madi passed, Rose had carried a lot of grief that tied her stomach in knots almost daily. To try to quell her nerves, she would ask Madi several times throughout each day how she was doing.

This evening was the first time Rose would receive a response.

"The second after I asked her how she was, my computer screen faded," she said. "Then the lamp faded. There was no dimmer on the lamp, and all the connections on the computer were fine. At first, I assumed we were having a power outage, but I looked into my bedroom across the hall and the lights were normal. The computer came back on after a few seconds, but then it dimmed again. The light had even more of a mind of its own, going from bright to dark to bright to dark, repeatedly. I got up and checked other rooms; everything electrical was working as it should have."

Nothing that was happening scared Rose; it puzzled her more than anything. But, after confirming that the rest of the house was in order, and after seeing her computer and light continue to do their own thing, she realized what was happening: she'd asked a question, and she was receiving an answer.

"I felt a presence, a really good feeling inside, and I knew it was my daughter," she said. "There was an energy around me that I had never felt before. It was very strong, very comforting. Then I had a feeling in my mind — like a voice, but not a voice. It was like when you suddenly recall a phone number or address. It was just a feeling of knowing, of knowing that it was Madi who was doing this. I felt a sense of happiness and peace that washed away my anxiety. She was letting me know that she heard me and that she was okay."

Rose said Madi wanted the family to celebrate that she was so happy now. "She didn't want us to miss her in the physical, because that wasn't her. She wanted us to know that no matter how difficult her life had been, she was released from all of that now. She was in a good place."

After Rose soaked in the energy and let the feelings she felt about Madi play out for several seconds, everything returned to normal.

"The lamp brightened and stayed bright, and the computer screen came on and stayed on," Rose said. "It was one of those moments that, when it's over, makes you say, 'Did that really just happen?' It *did* really happen, and it continues to bring me peace today."

Rose said it made sense that Madi sent her that sign when she did.

"It had been a few weeks since she had died, and I was miserable, with no end to that feeling in sight. There probably wasn't much she could have done to get my attention while I was talking to her earlier as I was cutting the grass, but it was easy with the computer and light. I am always in there working, so it was the perfect place for her to make me aware of her presence."

The computer and light have not faded or dimmed since.

"I think she told me what she needed to and what she knew I needed to hear. She calmed my fears. She knows now that I am going to be able to get through the difficult days. It was a very moving experience that put me on a path toward healing. And now I know that whenever I ask my baby girl how she is doing, she is really listening to me."

Would Madi have contacted her when she did if her mom had not asked her how she was doing? *I* believe she would have, since Rose was hurting so deeply from the loss and frequently talked to Madi. The office was the perfect place for them to connect because it was Rose's private space and had electrical devices to manipulate. By asking her daughter how she was doing, Rose was setting the intention. She wasn't just thinking about Madi; she was talking to her, even asking a question that only her daughter could answer.

When you find yourself thinking about a lost loved one, speak to them, be it in your mind or out loud. Invite them to enter your life and to communicate with you. Usually you will find that the more often you set your intention, the more obvious the signs will be.

15 The Power of Numbers

We encounter numbers all day, every day. Whether we're dealing with money, dates, or time, or even just changing the radio station or television channel, numbers are always in front of us. But sometimes a number, depending on its associations and the timing of it, can have meaning beyond face value. As frequent a role as numbers play in our daily lives, why *wouldn't* spirits use them to try to connect with us? They do, and one named Justin did so quite frequently with Judy.

When a relationship Judy was in had ended, her girlfriend in Florida suggested she get out of New Jersey for a while and fly south to spend some time with her.

"My flight got in late, but some friends of ours down there were night owls and told us to come over as soon as I arrived. A little while after we got to their house, a guy named Justin rolled in. It was about 1 AM and he had a bottle of champagne. I jokingly said, 'What, no caviar?' I spoke too soon; it was in his other hand."

After getting to know each other that evening, Justin asked her out. Judy said yes.

"We discovered that both of our previous relationships had ended on the same night. We really had a connection with each other. After I returned home, we stayed in contact with weekly letters and cards. We traveled by train, plane, and automobile to see each other. We eventually got engaged, we married a year later, and I moved to Florida. Our marriage lasted thirty-nine days short of five years."

Justin died from an infection. Judy was devastated, but she received some comfort soon after his death through various signs she knows came from her husband, including seeing someone who looked exactly like him, hearing songs that reminded her of him, and finding coins.

"At one of my readings with Bill, Justin came through and joked that I must have found twenty-five dollars in loose change since he had died," Judy said. "He was right, and the coins would always be significant based on the type, the year, or when I found them, such as a penny I came across the moment I was thinking about him that had the year he died on it, or a Canadian dime I found in my office at work just before I left to take a trip to Canada."

But it was when Judy decided to move to a new home after Justin passed that his presence burst through unlike any signs she'd ever experienced.

"We had been talking about moving before he died, and I decided that it was time," Judy said. "The day I started looking, there were two places in particular I made appointments to see based on their cost and the neighborhoods they were in."

She had the directions, but she hadn't given the numbers in the addresses any thought until she arrived at the first place.

When the address registered with her, she considered not even looking at the second place.

"The address was 51926," she said. "Justin was 51 years old when he died on September 26. I was absolutely certain that was a sign from him. How could those numbers be the address, and in that order? But since I already had an appointment to see the second place, I decided to look anyway."

When she got to the second residence, it was not only the numbers but also the street name that convinced her she couldn't go wrong picking either place.

"The address was 5426 Poppy. I realized that when you added the first two digits together, it was 926, the date he died. And poppies were the flowers we had chosen to have at our wedding. On top of that, orchids were actually Justin's favorite flower, and this house had beautiful orchids out front. There was no question that this was going to be my new home."

Not long after that, Judy flew to San Diego for the annual Soaring Spirits International convention, which is held for widows. "When I got to the hotel, the woman behind the desk gave me a choice of two rooms. I asked her what the room numbers were. Of course, one of them was 926."

On the final day of the convention, Judy was standing in line waiting to get a number for a 5K race she was about to run while in town. "I get up to the table and they give me my number. It was 51," she said. "There were hundreds and hundreds of people running this race. They were coming in by the busload. And somehow, out of every number I could have been given, they gave me that one."

No matter where Judy goes or what she does, the number 926 or 51 — or both — continues to pop up.

"The first night I slept in my new home, I cried," she said. "I thought because I had left the house he and I had lived in, I had in some way left him. But when I looked at it more from a spiritual perspective than a material one, I realized that that house we had was nothing more than a shell and that Justin had led me to this new one through the address. He was with me wherever I went. And that was proved again in San Diego with my room number and race number. I receive so many signs from him through numbers; they keep me comforted."

There is no question that numbers can be manipulated. Through addition, subtraction, division, and multiplication, you can probably come up with any combination you want in any situation. But when you consider that those same unique numbers continually appeared to Judy in some of the most emotional times of her life — when trying to find a new home after her husband's death and while at a convention for widows — it is difficult to deny that Justin, though gone from this earth, was still actively playing a significant role in the life of his true love, from the other side.

16 A Man by the Same Name

One of the best qualities a person can have when it comes to receiving signs is patience. They usually don't happen immediately, or when you want or expect them to. The more patient you are, often the greater the reward.

Johanna's father and her two uncles had passed away within a few years of each other. When she had come to me for a reading, her dad and one of her uncles came through very clearly, but the other uncle, Charles, did not. The only thing that came through that didn't make sense to her during the reading was the number 14. I was hoping that this number would somehow connect to Charles to give her some comfort that he, too, was okay, but she could not relate it to him or either of the other two men.

"I was really worried about my uncle Charles," Johanna said. "The three of them were brothers. It didn't make sense to me that two of them would come through and one wouldn't."

Johanna is a hostess at a fine-dining restaurant in a small

town in the Pacific Northwest. She works with customers face-to-face every day, many who are regulars and some who aren't. Two days after her reading with me, with her uncle on her mind, Johanna was working the register when a customer she'd never seen before came up to pay his bill.

"It was a typical transaction," she said. "We exchanged pleasantries, and he said his meal and the service were great. I ran his card through the machine, waited for the ticket to print, and had him sign it. Then we thanked each other, I gave him his copy, and he left."

Several seconds later, after the customer had walked out the door, Johanna took a closer look at the receipt.

"I don't always look at the receipts after I watch people sign them," she said, "but for some reason I looked at this one."

Her body trembled when she saw the man's name.

"I blurted out, 'Oh my gosh!' and ran out the door to chase him down. My boss probably thought I'd really messed something up when, in fact, everything was actually aligning perfectly, at least for me personally."

What made her take off after the man? His name: Charles Hankel.

"That was the name on the receipt, the name that was on his credit card," Johanna said. "That was my uncle's name, letter for letter. How many Charles Hankels are there in the world?"

She ran out the door and spotted him about to get in his car.

"I ran as fast as I could and was out of breath when I reached him, not so much from the distance I had to run but from the emotions I was feeling. My adrenaline was at an all-time high. When I got to him, I said, 'Mr. Hankel?' He said, 'Yes,' no doubt wondering why this crazy cashier was so frantic. I calmed myself down the best I could and explained to him that that was my uncle's name. I didn't tell him about my reading with Bill, because I didn't know how he'd react to that, but I did tell him my uncle had recently passed away and it just struck me that they had the same name."

Mr. Hankel's reaction blew Johanna's mind.

"He smiled at me and said, 'Wow, this really feels like something that was sent from heaven.' He had no idea…"

The two talked, and Johanna learned that he was from Louisiana. He was simply passing through town on vacation, and his visit to her restaurant was purely random — at least as far as he knew. The two exchanged email addresses, and Mr. Hankel went on his way.

"This was the validation I needed that my uncle was okay," she said.

But the validating was far from finished.

"When I emailed him later to thank him for coming into our restaurant and for talking to me, I noticed his middle name was part of his email address. Would you believe it was 'Christian'? My uncle's middle name was Kristian. Different spellings, but they sounded the same. It couldn't have gotten any better."

And yet, it did.

"I was mesmerized by that receipt with his name on it," Johanna said. "When I looked at it again even more closely, I couldn't believe my eyes."

Mr. Hankel had been sitting at table 14.

"Chills shot through me. I showed everyone at the restaurant, and I sent a picture of it to my grandma. These were her three sons. I could never bring them back for her, but I certainly was able to bring her some comfort with this."

Johanna's story offers a couple of good lessons about receiving messages and signs.

The first, which you have already seen in many of these stories, is that spirits can come up with some bizarre ways of communicating. As I stated when I discussed how they communicate with me, rarely do they say what they want to say in straightforward, black-and-white terms. Why Johanna's dad and other uncle were so direct and Charles wasn't, I do not know for sure. I can never guarantee who will come through in a session, and certain souls are quieter than others. This could have been a situation in which Charles wasn't shy, but he wanted to make a more lasting impression, which he obviously did. The answers we seek may not come through crystal clear or immediately. They can take time, patience, and a lot of focus on our part.

The other lesson is that we must trust what the spirits are saying to us, even if we don't initially understand it. So often I receive messages that don't make sense at the outset, but we have to trust that they will eventually. Johanna and I didn't know what "14" signified, or if it would even have anything to do with her uncle Charles, but there was no question that, in time, that number would mean something significant to her.

"Here I was, two days after my reading with Bill, wondering why I didn't hear anything from my uncle. Then some guy, who lives twenty-five hundred miles away in Louisiana and who shares my uncle's uncommon name, stops into our small-town restaurant on the day I'm working behind the register and pays with his credit card so I can see his name. Oh, and he happens to sit at table 14?

"Yeah," she said with a huge smile. "I'm confident my uncle is doing just fine."

17 "I Am Happier Than I've Ever Been"

I n the story about Phyllis and her dream about Mike, you read
that she had a gut feeling upon waking that something had happened to her former boyfriend. Further signs that day and an
eventual phone call from Mike's mother proved that her feeling
was accurate. But sometimes messages from spirits in dreams can
be even more direct. As you will read in this story, what a man
named Roger experienced in his dreams was an incredible gift
from his grandfather, the kind of vivid signs we all wish we could
have after a loved one passes.

Roger's grandfather was eighty-two years old and had cancer
when he died, so his death wasn't totally unexpected, but Roger
was still deeply saddened because the two were so close. A few
weeks afterward, Roger had the first of three dreams in which his
grandpa would visit him. These weren't dreams *about* his grandpa
but ones in which his grandpa actually appeared to him and, in
two of them, verbally communicated with him.

"I'd never experienced anything like them," Roger said. "I

knew I was dreaming while it was happening. I knew in each dream that I was asleep and that I was in the midst of a dream in which my grandpa was about to make an appearance and talk to me. The level of comfort and confidence I felt was indescribable."

In the first dream, Roger was sitting in a chair in his grandfather's living room. "My grandma and cousin and I were there," he said. "They were both crying as my grandpa's dead body lay on the couch, while I was excited with anticipation. Even though I knew he was dead, I knew that he was about to get up to talk to me. When he finally did rise from the couch after a few seconds, I guess my grandma and cousin couldn't see him, because they continued to cry and paid no attention to him. I was jubilant and said hi to him. He was very serious and just said, 'Come with me,' as he walked past me."

They went into the kitchen.

"He said that he didn't want my grandma to hear him say it, but she was going to need medication to combat depression because of how sad she was that he was gone. We then walked around the house, room by room, where he seemed to be making sure things were in order. Then we went outside, where a woman was backing his giant Cadillac out of the garage. I have no idea who she was, but when she backed out, she ran over his lawn mower. He turned to me, shaking his head with disgust, and said, 'Thank goodness I have your dad to take care of things while I'm gone.'"

The dream ended and Roger woke up.

"I felt wonderful, but I was also disappointed it was over," he said. "It was one of those moments that you wish would never end. I received a real visit from my deceased grandpa. I just wished that I had more time to talk to him."

Acting on the dream, Roger called his father the next morning and told him about what he had experienced. His dad was his grandmother's primary caregiver after his grandpa's death.

"I asked him if Grandma was on medication for depression. He said they had just gone to the doctor and gotten her some. Then I told him how grateful Grandpa was that he was taking care of Grandma. My dad was never much of a religious or spiritual person like I have always been, and he really struggled after my grandpa's death. There was no question, though, that what I told him had a significant impact on him. I realized that the dream probably wasn't so much for me as it was for him. I think my grandpa knew that I would be very receptive to him appearing to me, whereas it might have freaked out my dad a little bit if Grandpa had gone directly to him instead."

The second dream came a few weeks later and would be even more comforting. This time it opened with Roger in his grandpa's basement.

"It was a dark, old unfinished basement. The only reason I can figure why we were down there is because the rest of the family was upstairs being loud as they laughed and watched TV. The basement was a private place without any commotion. I was standing there by myself waiting for him to appear. I didn't know why he was coming, but I knew he was. After a few seconds, he was just there. Again, he looked very serious. We were staring at each other when I finally said, 'Hi, Grandpa. How are you?' He said, 'I am happier than I've ever been.'"

In his dream, Roger was so excited by his grandpa's response that he wanted someone upstairs to come down to hear it, too.

"I was yelling up to my sister. It was so loud up there that she couldn't hear me. And, for whatever reason, I knew that if I went up to get her, Grandpa would be gone when we got back. I didn't know what to do. But since I had heard what I had wanted to hear, I decided to take a chance. I ran up as fast as I could and told my sister to come down. She was having so much fun up there that she wouldn't listen to me. So, I ran back down myself and, sure enough, Grandpa was gone. I was disappointed, but I was overjoyed at the same time because he had told me what I wanted to hear. I called my sister the next morning after I woke up and let her know what she'd missed. She was sincerely apologetic. I laughed, but I do wonder what would have happened if, in the dream, she had come down and seen him."

The third dream was just days after the second one and lasted only a few seconds.

"I was awake late at night. I was in bed thinking about Grandpa and the dreams I'd had. As I was lying there, I asked him in my mind why he hadn't smiled at all in either of those dreams. 'You always seem so serious,' I said. 'Even though you said you were happier than you've ever been, there was no smile. It would be nice to see it in your face.' I wasn't being overly serious but just making a point to him as I was thinking about him. Soon after, I fell asleep and found myself in the same situation as the previous two dreams — I knew I was dreaming, and I knew he was about to show up."

This time, though, Roger wasn't anywhere in particular.

"I wasn't at his house or mine. It was like I was in an empty space staring straight ahead. Suddenly, just his face appeared right in front of me. He started out looking serious, but then he put his index fingers in his mouth, one on each side, and he stretched his mouth and stuck his tongue out at me. It lasted about two seconds and he was gone. I woke up laughing so hard that I was crying. He'd obviously heard my plea to look happy."

That would be the last time Roger's grandpa would appear to him in a dream.

"It has been seventeen years since he died, and just a little less than that since I had those dreams. I wondered for a long time why he never came back. I've asked him to return, but he never has. My wife and I moved a few months after those dreams, so I wondered if that had anything to do with it, but I don't think so. He had no real connection to my old house. I just think he said what he had to say, and he told my dad and me what we wanted to hear, and that was all that was needed — for him and for us."

Roger advised, "If anyone ever has a dream like those three — where you are being visited by someone who has died and you are fully aware that you are dreaming — embrace and take advantage of every second of it. Because even though it is a dream, it is a real connection to the other side. I have never felt anything like it since, and I may never again."

18 96 Tears

Another very common way for spirits to connect with us is through music. Almost as much as numbers, music is a part of our everyday lives. It is an easy way for spirits to reach us, assuming, of course, that we are paying attention.

When Amy and her family traveled to North Carolina one summer to visit her father-in-law, they made a side trip to South Carolina. It was a short excursion that meant the world to her because of the memories it brought back of her time with her own father, who was now deceased.

"I was eighteen and living in California at the time. Dad lived in Virginia. I went out to visit him for a couple weeks, and we decided to take a road trip to Charleston, South Carolina. We had the best time," she said. "We talked about life and our goals. I was more mature, and we had more 'relatable' conversations. We spent time walking the streets, going to the open-air market, and just bonding. I remember he told me how proud he was of me. Now, twenty years later, I was taking my own kids there."

Some time before her family vacation, when I had given Amy a reading and her dad had come through, he'd told me to tell her that he would give her signs through music. There was no specific song that he mentioned. Music in general was all I could share with Amy.

"I remembered as we were driving to South Carolina that Bill had said that," Amy said later. "So, I started to talk to my dad in my mind, asking him if he would join us in some way on this vacation. I didn't know what to expect or to look for. If the sign was going to be music, the only remote possibility I could think of was the song '96 Tears,' but I knew that probably wasn't going to happen, so I tried to keep my mind open to anything."

The song "96 Tears" was recorded by ? and the Mysterians. Yes, that was their real name; it started with a question mark. They were pretty much a one-hit wonder. They recorded "96 Tears" in 1966, it reached number one, and it was ranked by *Rolling Stone* magazine as one of the greatest songs ever.

"It was my dad's favorite song," Amy said. "I was born seven years after the song came out, so my dad taught it to me when I was little. We would sing along to it and laugh every time it came on the radio. I told my kids after he died that that was his song."

The family went to Fort Sumter, a sea fort in Charleston Harbor where the Civil War began. "After spending the day touring the island, we went back to the hotel to swim in the pool. It was a very small, quaint hotel. Nothing special. No frills. In the background there was some music playing. It was coming from a hotel speaker somewhere. It wasn't very loud, but we could faintly hear it playing one country song after another."

Until…

"My son yelled, 'Mom! Do you hear that?' I couldn't. I was

in the pool, where some kids were splashing, so I got out and listened.... 'Are you serious?' I exclaimed. I had to listen some more to make sure I'd really heard what I thought I heard. It made absolutely no sense. Coming out of that same speaker that had been spitting out nothing but country songs was '96 Tears.' We were at a small hotel on an island in the middle of the ocean after I had just asked my dad to join us on our trip, and that song comes on? The looks on the faces of my family were priceless. Honestly, I rarely hear that song on the radio because it's so old. In fact, I have it on my iPad because I know I have almost no chance of ever hearing it anywhere else. And, wouldn't you know it, as soon as it was over, they went right back to playing country music."

The family sang the song and laughed, just as Amy had always done as a little girl with her dad.

"I didn't hesitate to tell the kids that I had asked their grandpa to join us and that his spirit really was right there with us," she said. "There was no other logical explanation for a rock-and-roll song that was nearly fifty years old to suddenly play in the middle of those country songs. It just made everything on that trip that much better."

19 Preplanning a Sign

We are beings who love to plan. We plan our meals, we plan to meet up with friends, we plan our kids' activities, we plan our vacations. But have you ever thought of planning with someone how the two of you can communicate after one of you has died?

When Adrienne came to me for a reading, I could sense there was something going on with her grandfather, who was in his nineties. She explained to me that she and her daughter were living with him and that he had been ill for several years. I told her that he was fighting to stay alive because he was afraid to cross over to the other side for two reasons: he feared leaving her and her daughter alone, and he dreaded what awaited him on the other side, for he'd had many conflicts with his deceased sister and mother. I assured Adrienne that he could cross over knowing that everything here and there would be fine.

"After my reading, I told my grandfather that if he felt it was his time, then it was okay to go. I told him my daughter and I would be okay on our own, and I also threw in that he didn't have to be afraid of his mom or sister when he got to his next life. He laughed at that and said okay. Just three weeks later, he was gone."

Adrienne and her grandfather were spiritual people, and they talked for a couple of years about him sending her a sign from heaven.

"I told him when he was alive that after he died, I wanted a blue feather. I made it very clear that I didn't want dimes or other coins or anything simple like that. I wanted a blue feather. We live in Saskatchewan, Canada, an area where blue feathers are almost nonexistent. The only birds we have are pretty much ravens and seagulls. I figured if I ever found a blue feather, there would be no doubt that it came from him."

Adrienne had four sisters, two who were spiritual and two who were not at all. Arlinda was one who was not.

"When Arlinda would hear me tell my grandfather that I wanted to see a blue feather, she would say, 'Oh yeah, me too.' She was playfully mocking us, not really believing that she would ever see one."

After their grandpa died, guess who the first sister was to see a blue feather?

"Our family has a business that sells appliances," Adrienne said. "Four days after my grandfather's death, Arlinda walked behind the shop and found the most gorgeous, brilliant blue feather any of us had ever seen. When I told my grandfather to send blue feathers, I was thinking something small like from a blue jay. I don't know what kind of bird this one came from, but it had to be spectacular given the beauty of this feather. Arlinda was very emotional when she found it. She was so excited that she took a picture right away and sent it to all of us in a group message."

Less than a week later, Adrienne's other nonspiritual sister found a blue feather. It wasn't as vibrant as the one Arlinda had found, but a blue feather nonetheless.

"Now the two of them, the sisters who never believed, talk regularly about the signs they see," Adrienne said. "I never imagined when I asked my grandpa for this sign that it would change the lives of my two sisters who never believed. Now they believe as much as, if not more than, anybody."

So, when did Adrienne find *her* first blue feather?

"I still haven't," she said with a chuckle. "Can you believe that? But it's okay. I know he sent those feathers to them to raise their spiritual awareness, and it worked."

How much more validation could Adrienne want after watching her two sisters of little faith receive exactly what she and her grandfather had discussed? It's a rare and beautiful thing when you can plan something on this side and watch it come to fruition from the other side. The only word of caution I would throw in is to not limit yourself to looking for only a "preplanned" sign. We don't completely know how things work on the other side, so if you ask your grandfather for a blue feather before he dies but you don't receive one, it doesn't mean he isn't sending you other signs. Maybe, for whatever reason, a blue feather isn't going to be his sign to you, but something completely unrelated will be. Remember to keep your mind open to all possibilities.

20 708JPG

The primary effect receiving a sign from a loved one normally has on us is that it shifts our emotions from sadness and uncertainty to happiness and comfort. There may be no better example of that than what Catherine experienced.

Catherine and her husband, Jim, met in college. They married five years later and would have two beautiful boys. Sadly, six years into their marriage, they received the devastating news that Jim was diagnosed with stage IV colon cancer. He courageously fought it for nearly three years before passing away at the age of thirty-four.

Catherine is a person of faith, born and raised Presbyterian and a convert to Catholicism after marrying Jim. I had never met her, nor had I ever given her a reading. It was a friend who told me about her and two instances in which she had received significant signs from Jim. I tell you that to reinforce that you don't need me or anyone else to help you receive and recognize signs around you. All you need is a sliver of faith in something greater than us and an open mind.

"After Jim had died, I was introduced later that year to his childhood friend Jason. We'd never met prior to that, but I had heard so many stories about him from Jim that I felt in some ways I knew him. They had grown up together all the way through high school and were inseparable."

Catherine and Jason got along so well when they met that they began dating. It obviously was not initially easy for a recently widowed mother such as Catherine. She had to navigate through a lot of difficult emotions, but she received validation from Jim one day that he was supportive of her new beau.

"Jason and I had been dating for about a month when I was digging through a closet and found some random papers Jim had left behind," she said. "They were a bunch of letters I had written to him and cards I had given him during our thirteen years together. I wasn't surprised to find that Jim had kept them, but I was very surprised to find a card among them not from me."

Catherine said Jim never kept greeting cards from anyone except her.

"He'd open a card from someone and say, 'Oh, that's nice,' and then throw it away," she said. "So, to see that he kept a card from someone else was very odd. When I opened it, I recognized that it was a high school graduation card — from Jason's family."

Catherine was overwhelmed with emotion.

"I thought it was fascinating that the only card he ever kept was from them — not just from Jason but from his whole family. It made me feel good, that Jim would be okay with my new relationship. Nothing means more to me than our two boys, and

I knew Jim would approve of Jason and his family being part of our sons' lives."

While Catherine would continue to receive other small signs from Jim as time went on, there was one in particular she received in the fall that blew away all the others.

"The fall is always a difficult time for me because it was during that season when Jim's health really started to go downhill," Catherine said. "One evening, a couple of years after he'd died, I was going through all our winter coats and hats and gloves to get ready for the upcoming season. We live in Wisconsin, where the winters are brutal and the weather can go from mild one day to treacherous the next. I wanted to be prepared."

She hadn't expected the tide of emotions that came with the task. "I pulled out all the Green Bay Packers hats he'd collected, and I broke down crying. As a widow, you can have emotions rise to the surface oftentimes when you least expect them to. I'm sure I'd pulled these same hats out the previous year and didn't get emotional like this, but it was really rough this time. I finished going through them, and I cried myself to sleep that night."

The next morning, after getting her kids off to school, Catherine headed for work. Her feelings from the night before were lingering. Jim weighed heavily on her mind.

"I was driving the same route to work that I always had. It's not a very long distance, and I never encounter that many cars. It's a pretty quick and quiet ride."

She came to a stop sign. There was one car in front of her. "I was sort of in a daze and just happened to look right at the license plate," she said. "708JPG."

Jim's birthday was July 8. His initials were JPG.

"I was like, 'Seriously, you have to be kidding me.' And this was not a personalized plate. It was a standard, luck-of-the-draw plate that somebody in Wisconsin was given when they went to register their vehicle…and there it was right in front of me on the morning after my breakdown."

Catherine's mentality did a 180-degree turn. "That car was in the right place at the right time for my sake — Jim made sure of it," she said. "I went from feelings of sadness, and thinking about what our life together could have been if he were still alive, to 'Okay, I get it — you're still around.'

"I haven't felt detached from him since," Catherine continued. "Anytime I feel sad I think of that sign. It reminds me that no matter what we are going through, no matter how we feel, he is right there for me and our boys, and he always will be."

21 A Pond of Fish Beats a Pot of Gold

Have you ever seen the end of a rainbow? I never knew anybody who had until Nancy told me her story, which she knows was the work of her son.

Nancy's son, Jared, was twenty-six years old when he died suddenly in Colorado. Nancy, who lives in Mississippi, had seen her son just two days earlier when he returned home for her mother's funeral. Before moving to Colorado, Jared lived in a house owned by his parents that was seven miles from them.

"One day, seven months after he died, I went over to that house," Nancy said. "We hadn't done anything with it since he'd died; a lot of his stuff was still there. I went there just to be closer to him for a little while. I knew that he was in a much better place, but there is nothing as painful as losing a child. Anytime I felt that going over to that house and sitting in it for a while would make me feel closer to him, then that's what I would do."

After spending a couple of hours there, Nancy was ready to leave.

"I was on my way out the front door when I stopped and said, 'Jared, I know you're okay, but I'd like you to send me a rainbow so I know for sure that you are.' It was totally out of the blue. Rainbows had no significance to either of us. It's just what came out of my mouth. It even felt strange after I said it. On top of that, it was very hot and overcast, not the kind of day at all that you'd expect a rainbow to appear."

Nancy got in her car and headed home. It was approaching six in the evening. "It started to drizzle a little bit when I got close to home, but I honestly had already stopped thinking about a rainbow. And, like I said, it was so cloudy that there would have been almost no chance of one anyway unless the clouds really broke, and soon."

When Nancy got home, she started to cook dinner. She and her partner own a lot of land that includes a gorgeous fifty-acre lake behind their house. She was looking out the kitchen window when she noticed the rain had stopped. Though it was still overcast...

"I looked out and there it was — a rainbow," she said.

But, as you have read in many of the stories already, spirits often send more than one sign. Yes, it was fascinating that Nancy saw a rainbow soon after asking for it, but Jared wanted to make sure she was convinced it was from him.

"That rainbow — it had landed in the lake! I mean, the very end of the rainbow was in the lake," she said. "I honestly thought I was going crazy. I grabbed my camera and ran outside to take pictures as evidence. I thought I was hallucinating."

That lake was extremely significant in Jared's life. "He spent so much time there swimming and fishing," Nancy said. "I had seen countless rainbows in my life, but I had never seen the end of one. There was no pot of gold there, but there sure were a lot of fish. To Jared, fish were as good as gold.

"Even if I had thought it was going to rain that day and I had made that request for a rainbow to my son, who in the world would have thought it would end in the lake?" she continued. "It was such a meaningful sign, because it was not only what I had asked for at a very emotional time, but it happened in the place he loved the most growing up. I've seen a lot of rainbows since then and will probably see a lot more, but I doubt I'll ever see another one like that."

Nancy's story proves how oftentimes in our most dismal moments, all we need to do is ask for a sign from the other side and our prayers will be answered.

22 "Oh My Gosh, It's a Ghost!"

Anytime you receive a sign from a spirit, it is extremely likely you will know the one responsible for it and the meaning behind it. But there are rare occasions when a spirit may choose you to make themselves known for no reason other than convenience. As in Evelyn's story, that can be scary, exciting, and fascinating all at once.

Evelyn was a chaperone one day for her daughter's class field trip to their community's heritage park and museum. "The park and museum site is a jewel in our neighborhood that showcases our town's history," Evelyn said. "That day we walked to the museum, saw the exhibits, and walked back to school when we were finished. My daughter was about seven years old at the time."

After the field trip, the students were given a homework assignment that was based on the history of their community.

"My daughter and I were in what used to be our garage; we converted it into a playroom and office," Evelyn said. "She was working on the project and shouting questions to me while I was in the adjoining bathroom with my son, whom I was potty training. My multitasking was working quite well until some very loud music drowned out my daughter's voice."

Evelyn went into the playroom to find the stereo on at maximum volume.

"She looked at me all confused. I asked her what she did, and she said she didn't do anything; the stereo just came on by itself and got loud on its own. You know, because that's what stereos do, right? So, I shrugged it off, pushed the volume button down until the music was silent, and went back into the bathroom."

No sooner had Evelyn gotten to the bathroom than...

"It was loud again — all the way up!" she said. "My daughter was starting to get freaked out, insisting she didn't do anything. This time I turned the volume all the way down and pushed the power button to make sure it was off, then I headed back to the bathroom."

You can guess what happened next.

"Now I was getting irritated. I got my son off the toilet, got him dressed, and carried him on my left hip back to the blaring stereo. My daughter was hysterical. I didn't know what was going on. I pushed the volume down again and turned the power off again. I stayed there this time, staring down the stereo, just daring it to come back on with me watching."

And it did. "Right in front of my eyes!" Evelyn said. "I helplessly watched the digital volume bar go up from zero to ten...all the way up to the max of fifty. My daughter was screaming and covering her ears. The walls were shaking. The furniture was rattling. I turned it down and off again. The stereo switched on and up again. My son was still attached to my left side and laughing hysterically, like this was all some game he was in on. I yelled to my daughter, 'Where is the remote?' thinking that she must have been accidentally stepping on it. She pointed up to the shelf. There it was, out of her reach and my son's reach. Nobody was touching it, and nobody else was home."

Evelyn turned the stereo down and off one more time. She waited in silence for a few seconds. Then it kicked on again.

"I didn't know what else to do, so I instinctively screamed 'Please stop!' as loud as I could. And it did. Instantly. The volume went all the way down to zero. I had chills. How did I just do that?"

Her daughter freaked out. She screamed, "Oh my gosh, it's a ghost!"

Evelyn laughed and told her there was no ghost, that there had to be another reason. "Because that's what you tell a seven-year-old," she said. "But, in my mind, I knew there was no logical explanation for what had just happened. I was even thinking of the history of our house, and there really wasn't much. It was built around 2000 on top of what used to be lemon groves. Unless there were some angry dead lemons, we weren't living in the *Poltergeist* house."

Evelyn went to another room and called her husband.

"I was anxiously rambling nonstop, telling him everything that had happened. He tried to calm me down by telling me a neighbor was probably using a remote that triggered it. I just said, 'Chris, are you serious?' I know he was trying to find logic in what had happened, but there was none. I repeatedly turned the stereo down and off, and it repeatedly came back on the next instant. No way was a neighbor who couldn't even see us somehow turning it back on and up with perfect timing."

Chris always had been a skeptic.

"No way was he going to believe for a second that something supernatural had anything to do with this," she said. "He continued to tell me to calm down. I continued to freak out. After we hung up, my daughter and son and I got out of that room and worked on her school project in the kitchen. The stereo stayed quiet from that point forward."

About a week or two later, I was at someone's home giving a small-group reading. Evelyn was not part of the group, but she was there because she had brought a friend who was part of it. When it was over, Evelyn approached me and told me what had happened with the stereo. What follows is our conversation. It actually turned into a mini reading.

"Where did you go that day?" I asked her. "You went somewhere. To a museum, maybe?"

"Yes, we went to our heritage museum," she said.

"Tell me exactly where you went before and after."

"We walked from my daughter's school to the museum, saw the exhibits, walked back to her school, and then walked home to our house."

"That's it."

"That's what...?"

"You brought back a spirit from the museum," I said.

"What?" Evelyn exclaimed. "Are you out of your mind?"

I laughed. "Nope. I've seen this happen before. Did your daughter do something once you got home that related to the museum trip?"

"Yeah, she had a project to do on it."

"It makes perfect sense from the perspective of the spirit world," I said. "That project was something that the spirit was interested in, so he followed you home."

Evelyn was stunned, to say the least. I was even able to give her what I thought was the first name of the spirit — which, it turned out, matched the name of one of the town's founders.

"Bill said the spirit just wanted to get our attention to let us know he was there and interested in what we were doing. The project my daughter was working on was during his era. The stereo was a way he was able to communicate with us. Bill said he wasn't there to hurt us or to even scare us. That's why when I yelled at him to stop, he did. He wasn't angry. In fact, he was thrilled that we were doing what we were doing. It was the most fascinating story I had ever heard."

Evelyn's husband has become a believer himself. And she now recognizes signs all the time, especially from her recently deceased grandmother.

"My entire family feels my grandma's presence," Evelyn said. "We actually talk about it every time we see each other, asking each other what signs we have received from her."

This story is a bit unusual compared with the others in that Evelyn wasn't asking for a sign and didn't even know the person who was trying to give her one. For a spirit to "latch on" to someone and go home with them is rare, but when it does happen, there is always a logical explanation why the spirit did it.

This spirit in particular was very gracious, thankful for their visit to the museum and for their project, and he simply wanted to be part of it. And when they acknowledged his presence and asked him to stop, he did, a good example of the fact that spirits will listen to us when we make our voices heard by them. This project probably brought the spirit a lot of happiness, and it also gave Evelyn and her daughter a really good story to tell.

23 A Cameo Appearance Abroad

Time is irrelevant on the other side, which is why I always encourage those seeking signs to be patient. Spirits also don't care *where* you are. For example, a spirit may die in America and you may live in America, but it doesn't mean that they can't send you a sign if you happen to be abroad, as Denise learned.

I did a phone reading with Denise, and her deceased brother, Glenn, was coming through. After she was able to validate that it was him by things he was telling me about himself, I informed her that he was going to be on a train with her in the next couple of days. This message was coming through very clear.

She was astounded — and puzzled. She said, "My reading with Bill was the day before I was leaving for Japan, where we were going to see my daughter to celebrate her birthday. I hadn't told him I was traveling anywhere. And, yes, I would be on a train in Japan. But I didn't know what he meant when he said my brother would be on the train with me. When I asked, he said it would be like a visitation, maybe someone who looked like him. Bill was very certain about this."

Denise and her husband arrived in Japan and checked into their hotel on a Thursday evening. On Friday morning, when they exited the elevator in the lobby to head to the train station for a trip to Kyoto, Denise received a surprise. Her brother was there in the hotel! I guess he simply couldn't wait for her to get to the train. This kind of thing happens at times. When spirits present me with information, it can come in so quickly that it's not always cohesive. I knew there was a train involved and I knew her brother would show up, but the order of events was out of sequence.

"We were getting off the elevator when, off to the side in this absolutely enormous hotel lobby packed with people, I noticed a man sitting in an upholstered chair. I completely froze. Fortunately, he wasn't staring at me the way I was at him, because I don't know how I would have reacted if we had made eye contact. It was Glenn."

It wasn't really Glenn, of course, though her brother was certainly responsible for that moment.

"I couldn't stop staring!" Denise said. "He even had the same expression on his face that Glenn used to have. This man was trying to read something or figure something out, and he looked quizzical in exactly the same way Glenn did sometimes.

"Have you ever seen an Alfred Hitchcock movie? You know the way Hitchcock would slip himself briefly into a public scene as a cameo? It felt like that. It wasn't scary, though — not at all. Actually, it was quite comforting. And what was amazing was how he was positioned in a place where I couldn't miss him as I walked off the elevator. That lobby was bigger than any I'd ever seen. If he were just about anywhere else, I never would have noticed him."

A sign like that the day after a reading is normally enough for one person, but there was more in store for Denise. A couple of years earlier, when I had given Denise a reading, I had told her that dragonflies would be a symbol of her deceased father and, actually, of that entire side of the family. She had seen dragonflies before outside her home, but nothing like she was about to encounter.

"We had a suite on the outskirts of Kyoto, the thirty-third floor of a skyscraper hotel. I was in the bedroom when my daughter and husband suddenly called for me to get into the living room. I ran in to find a swarm of dragonflies outside the window. According to my daughter, there were at least five hundred of them. According to my husband, there were at least a thousand. In either case, suffice it to say, there were more dragonflies than any of us had ever seen in one place in our lives. They hovered there for about ninety seconds and then flew away directly toward Lake Biwa. They did not pay any visits to other floors of the hotel after ours. It was one of the strangest and, at the same time, most comforting things I have ever seen."

I mentioned a while back that sometimes what may appear to be a sign isn't *really* a sign. If you visit a swamp that you know dragonflies are likely to inhabit, it probably wouldn't be right to assume they are a sign. However, when you suddenly see a swarm of them hovering for a minute and a half outside your thirty-third-floor hotel window in Japan, you should feel confident knowing that someone on the other side had something to do with it.

And one more thing…

"We took a walk along Lake Biwa later that day," Denise said. "While we were there, a tourist boat passed us. It was called *The Michigan*. Yeah, a tourist boat in the middle of a lake in Japan called *The Michigan*."

Denise and her brother grew up in Michigan, and she and her husband live there.

24 From Discouragement to Delight

The personality of a spirit will generally be the same one they had in human form. For example, if a person is shy and quiet on earth, they will be shy and quiet from the other side, possibly making it a little more difficult for that spirit to send signs. Of course, if that person was outgoing on earth, the signs coming from them in spirit could be obvious and plentiful.

Pam has lived in her current home in Massachusetts for twenty years. For about the first nineteen of them, she'd never had an electrical issue. The wiring had been updated. The bulbs were standard. But that changed when she returned home from Connecticut after her mom died.

"I noticed that a light went out. Okay, no big deal," Pam said. "But then another one went out. And another. And another. I had the electrical checked. Nothing was wrong, they said. Then the lights upstairs would flicker, go dim, and then brighten."

That was just the beginning.

"My son, Nicholas, heard a noise in my office in the middle

of the night. He found that my printer was on — and everyone else in the house was sound asleep. It was making that *eeeent-eeeent-eeeent* noise, as if it was printing something, but no paper was coming out. When it stopped, he went back to his room, where a lantern dimmed and then brightened. I'm not sure he slept well that night. We had no explanation for what was happening."

Pam came to me soon after for a reading.

"Once I spoke with Bill," she said, "I absolutely knew that my mom was behind all of it. She and I had a very strong bond, and this was her way of letting me know that she was with us. So, what had been inexplicable and even a little scary became very warm and comforting. When the lights would flicker or the printer would kick on by itself after that, I'd just say 'Hi, Mom' and they would stop, which confirmed for me that Bill was right. It was good to know that even though she was on the other side, she was still with us too."

Pam's mother also had a very strong bond with Nicholas, and it continued after her death.

"Nicholas recently started his freshman year in college. It was a big step that included a lot of adjustments for the entire family. He is majoring in history and hopes to become a teacher, which is what my mom was for so many years. She was so happy when he told her before she died that he would be going into that field. He is also minoring in theater, which is his true passion, but he knows that teaching is much less competitive in the job market."

One of Nicholas's first auditions was for the play *Twelfth Night*. "He called me afterward, and I could tell by his voice something was wrong. It was cracking, like he was on the verge of tears. He told me he completely choked during his audition; his mind had gone blank after a couple of sentences. When the words just wouldn't come to him, he took a bow and left the stage. He was so distraught. I spoke to him at length trying to encourage him, but also to help him understand that life, unfortunately, does come with disappointments. After we were finished talking, he told me he was going to walk over to the café to see if he could meet up with some friends."

About fifteen minutes later, Pam's phone rang.

"It was Nicholas. His voice had completely changed; it was full of excitement. I thought that he'd somehow gotten the part, but that wasn't it at all. He said as he was walking to the campus café feeling down and asking himself why this had happened, he looked up to see the streetlamp flickering, just like the lights and lantern in our home. It was repeatedly flickering, dimming, and then becoming the brightest white glow you could imagine. In fact, he was standing there watching it go through that cycle while he was on the phone with me. He eventually blew a kiss up to the sky and said, 'I love you, Grandma.' Now I was the emotional one."

Pam had tears in her eyes listening to Nicholas tell this story.

"I know that was truly a sign from my mother to make Nicholas feel better and to encourage him to never give up," she said. "To hear the complete delight in my son's voice after he was so down and discouraged just minutes before, and all because of my mother's sign from the other side, made me so happy. My mom faced many challenges in her ninety-one years of life on earth, and I always admired her strength, courage, and unending willpower. I think that may be why it is almost 'easy' for her to come through with the signs we see so frequently, no matter where we are."

I would agree that a woman with that kind of personality probably finds little difficulty sending signs to this side.

I'm always touched when someone shares a story like this with me. Knowing, through signs, that their loved one is around them brings solace, easing the heaviness of what seems like the finality of death. When we remain open to these little signals from spirits, we can rest assured that there is more waiting for us as we pass from this life to the next, and we can be comforted that the ones most important to us are still around us, just in a different form.

25 Running with Angel(s)

The title of my first book, *Expect the Unexpected*, conveys what I encounter in my work daily. It also reflects the notion that you will normally receive a sign when you least expect it, as Paul found out.

Paul was into physical fitness, including running. He lives across the street from a beach in Southern California, and a few times a week he would run the four-mile trail built alongside it. But, one day, an injury forced him to the sidelines.

"I hurt my knee somehow," he said. "I don't know what I did to it. There may have been just too much stress on it. It started to hurt one day, and the pain became unbearable for a while. I had to stop running until it healed itself."

It took a good year before it felt completely better.

"But, after that year, I couldn't get myself to run," he said. "I had gained a lot of weight during the injury, and I had lost my motivation. In fact, I pretty much stopped working out altogether."

Paul wasn't much of a believer in anything spiritual until we met and he had some readings with me. After that, he began to pray a lot, and he developed a strong relationship with God.

"I decided I needed to do something about my weight; I couldn't continue to live like this. So, I made up my mind when I woke up one morning that I was immediately going to start running again, and I did."

When he started out on that four-mile trail, it was difficult, as expected. "I prayed a lot to God as I ran, asking him to show me signs that would give me the strength to keep going. And then this kid ran right past me."

That kid, as Paul would later learn, was a high school junior he had never seen on the trail before. It was obvious they had something in common: they were both overweight.

"But he blew right by me, like I was standing still," Paul said. "As soon as I saw him, I remember saying to God, 'What kind of sign is that?' I had asked for the strength to do this. Watching some young kid zoom past me like that wasn't helping."

Paul continued to run at a slow and steady pace. "I didn't care how long it took me; I just wanted to do the entire four miles."

Soon after that kid had passed him, Paul came upon him again. The kid had stopped and was breathing heavily.

"I ran past him, but I was ahead for only a minute," Paul said. "The next thing I knew, he was sprinting right by me again, leaving me in his dust. I'm thinking, *Seriously, not only is this not helping me, but it's the opposite of the encouragement and strength I was hoping for.* I would eventually pass him again a couple more times as he stopped to catch his breath, but each time he'd come back and dart right by me. It was like the tortoise and the hare. He would sprint as fast as he could, I would jog at a pretty slow pace, and we'd keep passing one another. But each time he'd pass me it was like he was a world-class sprinter. I felt like I would have been better off being there by myself."

Paul continued to push forward both mentally and physically despite continually being passed by an overweight teenager. He eventually made it through the entire trail.

"When I finished what was the most difficult four miles I'd ever run, someone tapped me on the shoulder. I turned around and it was that kid."

"That was impressive," he said to Paul.

"What? What are you talking about?" Paul replied.

"How were you able to run so long without stopping even once?"

"Are you kidding? I was wondering how you were able to keep racing past me so fast every time," Paul said.

"That's easy when you have to keep stopping," the kid said to him. "What you just did was impressive. I hope to be able to do that one day."

Those words reversed Paul's perception.

"I realized that my prayers had actually been answered," he said. "I felt like I was the one struggling as I was watching him, yet he felt the same way about me. We both had weight issues, and we were both out there to make ourselves healthier. We just had two different approaches. I realized then that God probably gave us each other that morning. And that feeling was confirmed for me when the kid told me his name."

It was Angel.

"Every single time I ran before my injury, I would dedicate my run to someone in my life who had died," Paul said. "I would think about them as I ran, and it motivated me to keep going.

That morning, maybe because I hadn't run for so long, I forgot to dedicate that run to anybody. I think Angel was sent to me by God that day not only for the sake of our shared desire to get fit, but to remind me that those on the other side — those angels, whom I had dedicated my runs to in the past — really were with me. After that day, I would get in the habit again of not only running regularly but dedicating each run to someone I'd loved and lost."

26 Cookie

This story, from my assistant, Zaul, is a little more personal than the others because it involved me in a way I was initially unaware of. It is so simple, funny, and fascinating all at once that I felt compelled to share it.

Zaul has worked for me for the past seven years. He is not only an employee but a very good friend. He also runs his own catering business, as cooking is his first love.

"I had an older truck that I used to deliver our food, but it kept giving me problems," Zaul explained. "It would break down, I'd get it fixed, and then it would break down again. Mechanics couldn't figure out a long-term solution. It was causing me a tremendous amount of anxiety each day because I couldn't afford a new vehicle, but I also couldn't afford to have this one break down on me during a job or I'd lose my business."

One evening, Zaul was sitting on his couch watching television — the drama *Empire*, to be exact. "There's a character on the show named Cookie Lyon, played by Taraji P. Henson. I like Cookie a lot because she has a lot of fire and passion, which reminds me of my mom."

Zaul's mom died in 1999 when he was in his early twenties.

"I was really stressed about what to do regarding my truck, wondering if it would allow me to fulfill my next catering job. At the same time, I was watching this show, which got me thinking about my mom and how much I missed her. With all this weighing on my mind, I started talking to my mom. I asked her to send me a sign that would let me know she was with me and that everything regarding my truck and my business would work out."

But Zaul didn't ask for just any sign.

"I was also texting with Bill while I was talking to her and watching the show," Zaul said. "I said to my mom, 'I want you to have Bill text me the word *cookie*. That will be your sign to me.'"

As I've stated, asking for or watching for a specific sign from a spirit can cause us to miss other obvious signs. Could his mother send him a sign when he asks for one? Of course. Could she somehow make me use a random word like that with her son when he asks for it? That seems a bit over-the-top, even I have to say. While setting the intention is good, making such a specific request could result in disappointment.

"Did I think she would send me that sign through Bill?" Zaul said. "The word *cookie*? Really? No, I didn't think that at all. It's not that I didn't believe, because I did. I had received many signs from her and other loved ones who had passed. But I knew it was kind of ridiculous to tell her that I wanted something that specific. I was just very frustrated with my situation and was hoping for something a little more convincing to pick me up."

Zaul and I continued to text each other for a little longer before wrapping up our conversation. He told me he'd talk to me the next day.

"Bill texted back," Zaul said. "I expected his response to be 'See you tomorrow' or 'Have a good night' or 'Sounds good' or even just 'Okay.' But what did it say? It said 'cookie.' No joke. It really said 'cookie.' I'd have fallen down if I hadn't been sitting."

Within seconds after I had sent that text, my phone rang. It was Zaul.

"I said, 'Bill, why did you just send me that?' He was confused and asked me what I was talking about. I said, 'Cookie! Why did you text me the word *cookie*?' He laughed at me. He said, 'I never said that.' I said, 'Yes, you did. I have it right here on my phone.' Bill looked at his phone and busted out laughing again."

I hadn't typed "cookie." I'd typed "coolio" — as in, when he told me he'd see me tomorrow, I was whimsically saying "cool." But the spell-check feature on my phone didn't recognize the word, so it autocorrected it, turning the *l* into a *k* and the last *o* into an *e*, to change the message from *coolio* to *cookie*.

"I told Bill what had just happened, and he was really excited," Zaul said. "Not as excited as I was, but pretty darn excited. He said, 'Seriously, Zaul, could anyone ever receive a better sign than that?' I've learned from Bill that signs don't normally come to us in the way we expect or at our request. But to receive something that exact, just minutes after asking for it, was truly a gift, a gift from my mom."

Zaul's truck was able to last long enough for him to purchase another one, and his catering business continues to flourish today.

"I knew after receiving that text that everything was going to be okay. I didn't know yet *how* things would be okay, but it strengthened my faith and gave me hope that they would be. The shock of seeing that one word significantly lessened the stress at hand and triggered a huge sigh of relief. It raised me up, which was exactly what I needed at that time in my life."

27 A Sign from a Funeral

Every sign we receive from a spirit is a gift unlike any other. That is why it is so important to be able to recognize it when it is presented to us, as James did during a very emotional situation he was involved with.

There was a horrific traffic accident one day. Several high school students in an SUV were driving home from spring break when they were forced off the road by a semi, causing their vehicle to flip several times. All but one of the students survived. Jenna was pronounced dead at the scene. She was a model student, a senior set to graduate in a month and go to college in the fall. She left behind her mother, father, and two siblings.

James was a journalist for the local paper. "I had covered some pretty difficult stories over the years, but this was as tragic as anything I'd ever had to write about," he said. "I think it hit me hard personally because I had three kids of my own, the oldest of whom was in middle school. I couldn't imagine what Jenna's parents were going through."

James's initial coverage was based on police reports and comments from school administrators. But then, two days after the accident, one of his sources asked him if he'd like to speak with Jenna's father.

"I was told that he was willing to speak only to me because my source had said some nice things to him about my reporting," James said. "It was one of those interviews that I really wanted to do, and I had to do, but at the same time I *didn't* want to do it because of the emotions involved."

James arranged the meeting for that afternoon at Jenna's house.

"I knocked on the door and her father answered. He was the only one there, at least that I could see. I shook his hand and told him how sorry I was. He thanked me and took me through the house to the back porch. We talked, laughed, and cried for about an hour. He didn't want to discuss the details of the crash. He just wanted to talk about how wonderful his daughter was and how important it was to keep her legacy alive, and I obliged. It was a very surreal interview. I sensed he was still in a state of shock."

The funeral was a couple of days later. James was there to report on it.

"It is difficult covering stories like this because you want and need to be respectful while still doing your job," he said. "I brought a pen and a single piece of paper that I folded a couple of times to make as small as possible, and I kept them in my pocket. I stood in the corner in the back of the church and only pulled them out when I needed to quickly make note of something that I thought I might forget. I kept most of the notes, though, in my head."

Next to where James was standing was a large poster of Jenna. "The entire service was the saddest event I'd ever been to. I kept looking at that poster, with Jenna's bright, smiling face, and I couldn't stop thinking of my oldest son. He was also very bright and happy, and not far from starting high school. I was imagining how I would react if this had happened to him. People may ask why I would do that, but I'm an empathizer. I could never feel what Jenna's dad had felt, but I felt I had a duty to at least try. Not just as a reporter, but as a father."

Throughout the service, James continued to think about his son, who was only a few miles away going about his normal day at school, just as James was at his job, while Jenna's family was saying goodbye to their daughter and sister.

"After the service, I walked outside and noticed some girls from Jenna's school, each holding a bowl that people were dipping their hands into. I went up to one of the girls to ask what it was. She said each bowl contained three hundred sixty-five slips of paper, each with a different date. They were asking each person to pull one out and to pray for Jenna and her family every year on that date. I thought it was a novel idea, something I had never seen before."

The girl asked James to pull out a date.

"I always had a personal rule in reporting that I would never make myself part of the story I was covering. For example, if I was covering a story involving food, I would not accept any of the food if offered. For this story, I stood inconspicuously in the back of the church and didn't let my note-taking be noticed, and all I needed to know was what the girl was doing with the bowl. I didn't have to pull out a date for myself. But this was different. This whole story was different from anything I'd ever covered.

I became emotionally involved when I interviewed Jenna's dad, and I decided there was no reason not to pull out a slip of paper. So, I reached in and took one."

The girl asked James what date he got.

"I was speechless," James said. "I looked at her and knew that if I had tried to answer her, I would have cried. I just turned and showed her. She smiled and said, 'Oh, May 20.' That date meant nothing to her, of course, but to me — it was my oldest son's birthday.

"I don't know who was responsible for that happening, but I know it wasn't by chance," James continued. "I never knew Jenna personally, so I don't believe it came from her, but I do believe that it came from a spirit who knew me, who knew how much I was thinking of my son that entire week and how fortunate I felt to not be experiencing the pain that Jenna's family was going through. Now, every year on my son's birthday, it's more than just singing to him or eating cake or getting him a gift. I think about Jenna, too, which reminds me how much of a gift my son is to me."

Epilogue: Awareness

It has been said that if you see the time 11:11 on a clock, it means angels or spirits are present, something I firmly believe. It means they are watching over you, guiding you, encouraging you to pay attention to your intuition. I once told this to a friend, who had never heard of such a thing. Since then, he says, a few times a week on average he happens to glance at the clock to find that it is 11:11, and it brings him a tremendous amount of comfort.

Think about that for a moment. The time 11:11 occurs just twice a day, and for just sixty seconds on each occasion. My friend is normally in bed before 10:30 PM, so for him it usually happens only once daily. If he is awake for about sixteen to seventeen hours a day (roughly a thousand minutes), his chances of seeing 11:11 when he glances at the clock on any given day are about one in a thousand. And to recognize it a few times a week seems implausible — unless, maybe, there is some divine intervention in play.

What many people don't understand is that this sign from the spirit world didn't start being sent to my friend after I told him about it. I can assure you he saw 11:11 many times before he knew its spiritual meaning. So, what is the difference between then and now?

Awareness.

Everything I have discussed and every story you have read in this book comes down to awareness. Each of us has an antenna that can pick up energy and information from the spirit world all day and every day. The issue is whether we tune out the distractions of this world, and tune in to and recognize that information and energy the antenna is attracting. We all have the capability to tune in at a deeper level, but we need to have that awareness to do it. It's like a radio. Each one has an antenna to pick up signals, but the power button needs to be turned on for it to work.

Before I conduct a reading with someone, I shift my awareness from the outside world to my inner self, usually through meditation. It's like a shift in my present reality. When I am able to focus on my antenna and tune out the chaos around me, I become more aware of that which is spiritual and less aware of the worldly side of life.

The ability to do this is there for everyone, but it takes practice and patience. Some people are so eager to feel the spirits that, if it doesn't work in ten minutes, they get frustrated and quit trying. It takes time. It's a process. For some, yes, it can take just minutes. For others, it can take days, weeks, months....

Once those in the spirit world know that you have opened your heart and mind to them, they will do everything they can to reach out to you and make their presence known. I have found that most spirits will try to be as obvious and make their signs as evident to you as they possibly can. But you must stay open to whatever they present to you. Many people fail to recognize signs because they aren't seeing what they want or expect to see.

As I have repeatedly emphasized, you have to be alert to all possibilities. If your deceased father was an airline pilot and you are focused on looking for signs that relate to aviation, you may miss your dad's doppelgänger who just walked past you in the store, or you may not recognize an object right in front of you that was significant to both of you when he was alive. There is no limit on the possibilities for what the signs might be.

Why do spirits send us signs? To try to guide us in our daily lives. To help us choose the right paths. To bring us closer to one another. The greatest overall message I have received from the spirit world over the years is that we are here to experience love with each other. The spirits want us to stay connected through love. This life goes by in the blink of an eye — nobody knows that better than they do. They can see the truth of that much more from their perspective now than they could when they were here, because they no longer have the earthly distractions that they once had and that we still have. Be open to them; they know exactly what they are doing.

If you are still skeptical or not sure you can make this work, I encourage you to try it. Shift your thinking. Believe that spirits are around you. Believe that they are trying to communicate with you. Believe that they are as alive today as they were before they went to the other side, just in a different form.

French philosopher Pierre Teilhard de Chardin is credited with saying, "We are not human beings having a spiritual experience. We are spiritual beings having a human experience." His quote has always resonated with me. Life is a beautiful journey, and although it is temporary, it does not end; death is merely a transition. If you keep that mind-set, you will not be able to deny the presence of spirits in your life today. The signs — the proof — are everywhere, but you must remain open to seeing them. Only then will you receive the message that our inner light can never be extinguished.

Acknowledgments

I want to give special thanks to my family and friends, whose unwavering support over the years has had tremendous and significant meaning to me.

Thank you to all the phenomenal people at New World Library for believing in me and supporting the ideas I had for this book; especially to Georgia Hughes for giving me this opportunity and for all your love and support during this process; and to Kim Corbin for your continuous dedication to getting the word out.

I want to send a humongous thank-you to William Croyle for really understanding how to help me put into words what I am thinking and for bringing this whole thing together.

Thank you to everyone who took the time to share your stories in this book. Your acknowledgment of Spirit is the validation that others need to know that there is life on the other side.

Thank you to Melissa (MC) Cubillas, who has been a huge support and friend along this journey. I want to acknowledge Zaul Hernandez for everything he has done for me over the years to keep my life in order and for being someone who "gets" me, whom I can trust, and who is there whenever I need him.

I want to thank my partner, Patrick Markert, for being my rock, for grounding me, for making me laugh, for making this whole process just downright fun for me, and for using his gift of writing to advise me — it has been invaluable. And, of course, I cannot forget to thank my dogs, Teddy and Balto, my little fur babies, who bring love and joy to my life and who remind me to live in the present as they do.

Lastly, I want to thank my mom, Yvonne, who has half of my heart with her on the other side. Without her, none of this would be possible. I feel you here with me, guiding me, inspiring me, and flooding me with the light of your love. Because of you, I can share with others the message of how to recognize that the ones we love are always with us.

About Bill Philipps

B ill Philipps is a psychic medium who helps the deceased communicate with their loved ones on earth. Bill's fresh, upbeat, and direct approach perfectly complements his warm and relatable demeanor, captivating audiences worldwide.

Bill studied opera at the San Francisco Conservatory of Music and graduated in 2008. He found that music, in a deeply spiritual way, enabled him to tune in to and further develop his psychic-medium abilities, which dated to his childhood. He gave readings while attending the Conservatory and, after graduating, professionally pursued his true calling.

Bill's guidance is sought by many, including top executives, celebrities, and everyday people, who are all looking for common answers about life and the afterlife. Bill has appeared on many shows, such as *Dr. Phil* and *Access Hollywood*. He conducts individual readings in person, by phone, or via Skype. He also offers small-group readings and large-audience readings throughout the United States. He lives in Southern California. You can learn more about Bill at www.billphilipps.com.

About William Croyle

Coauthor William Croyle is a native of Cleveland, Ohio, and a graduate of St. Ignatius High School and Ashland University. He is the author of nine other books with some of the world's most inspirational people. He lives in Erlanger, Kentucky, with his wife, Debra, and their three sons. More information on his books is available at www.williamcroyle.com and at www.facebook.com/williamcroylebooks.